NO BOUNDARY

9
14

NO BOUNDARY

*Eastern and Western Approaches
to Personal Growth*

Ken Wilber

WITHDRAWN

SHAMBHALA
Boston
2001

To Jack Crittenden
Best student, best teacher, best friend

SHAMBHALA PUBLICATIONS, INC.
Horticultural Hall
300 Massachusetts Avenue
Boston, Massachusetts 02115
www.shambhala.com

© 1979, 2001 by Ken Wilber

9 8 7 6

Printed in the United States of America
⊗ This edition is printed on acid-free paper that meets the
American National Standards Institute z39.48 Standard.
Distributed in the United States by Random House, Inc.,
and in Canada by Random House of Canada Ltd

Library of Congress Cataloging-in-Publication Data
Wilber, Ken.
No boundary.
Reprint. Originally published: Los Angeles:
Center Publications, 1979. (Whole mind series)
Includes bibliographies and index.
1. Consciousness.   2. Self-perception.
3. Psychology—Philosophy.   4. East and West.
I. Title.   II. Series: Whole mind series.
[BF311.W577 1981]   158'.1   81-40489
ISBN 0-394-74881-6 (pbk.)   AACR2
ISBN 1-57062-743-6

Contents

Preface to the 2001 Edition

A LTHOUGH *No Boundary* is the second book I wrote, almost thirty years ago, it is still one of the most popular of my books. I believe the reason is simple: *No Boundary* was one of the first books to present a "full-spectrum" view of human potentials, potentials that reach from matter to body to mind to soul to spirit, and in so doing, it integrated the very best of psychology with the best of spirituality. In drawing on the finest of both Eastern and Western approaches to human growth and development, it charted a complete spectrum of consciousness that moved from subconscious to self-conscious to superconscious, from prepersonal to personal to transpersonal, from instinct to ego to God. And it offered an entire smorgasbord of actual practices and exercises that showed the reader how to reach each of these higher states of consciousness. The completeness of this approach made it rather unique, and I believe that is why readers have continued to respond enthusiastically.

The years since I wrote *No Boundary* have convinced me even more that its basic message is still sound and true. Human beings do indeed possess a remarkable spectrum of consciousness, a vast rainbow of extraordinary potentials and possibilities, and those potentials do indeed run from matter to body to mind to soul to spirit. Individuals can grow and develop through that entire spectrum, directly experiencing each of those "levels" or "colors" in the rainbow, resulting in a direct experience of spirit itself. Various psychological and spiritual practices—many of which you will be offered in the following pages—help us directly experience these various levels or waves in our own being. Thus, using a combination of these practices can help us fully awaken to every color in the rainbow of our own being, to every level of consciousness in the entire spectrum, and thus awaken to our real nature and true condition—an awakening known as "enlightenment," "release," or "the great liberation."

No Boundary was a popular version of the first book I had written, a large, somewhat academic book called *The Spectrum of Consciousness*. Those books would form the foundation of the almost twenty books that would follow. I would of course refine and polish the various points, but the essentials—such as the spectrum of consciousness itself—are still much as presented here, which is probably another reason this book has remained so popular. If you enjoy *No Boundary* and would like to see some of these further refinements, you might start with an overview of my current work, called *A Theory of Everything: An Integral Vision for Business, Politics, Science, and Spirituality*.

In the meantime, the basic message of *No Boundary* is just what the title says: your own basic awareness—and your very identity itself—is without boundaries. Your basic identity spans the entire spectrum of consciousness, from matter to body to mind to soul to spirit, and thus in the deepest or highest part of you, you embrace the All. What follows is a simple guidebook to this extraordinary territory of your own true selfless Self.

K.W.
Summer 2000
Boulder, Colorado

NO BOUNDARY

1

Introduction: Who Am I?

S UDDENLY, WITHOUT ANY WARNING, at any time or place, with no
apparent cause, it can happen.

> All at once I found myself wrapped in a flame-colored cloud.
> For an instant I thought of fire, and immense conflagration
> somewhere close by in that great city; the next, I knew that the
> fire was within myself. Directly afterward there came upon me
> a sense of exultation, of immense joyousness accompanied or
> immediately followed by an intellectual illumination impossible
> to describe. Among other things, I did not merely come to be-
> lieve, but I saw that the universe is not composed of dead matter,
> but is, on the contrary, a living Presence; I became conscious in
> myself of eternal life. It was not a conviction that I would have
> eternal life, but a consciousness that I possessed eternal life then;
> I saw that all men are immortal; that the cosmic order is such
> that without any peradventure all things work together for the
> good of each and all; that the foundation principle of the world,
> of all the worlds, is what we call love, and the happiness of each
> and all is in the long run absolutely certain. (R. M. Bucke)

What a magnificent awareness! We would surely be making a grave
error if we hastily concluded such experiences to be hallucinations or
products of a mental aberration, for, in their final disclosure, they share
none of the tortured anguish of psychotic visions.

The dust and the stones of the street were as precious as gold, the gates were at first the ends of the world. The green trees when I saw them first, through one of the gates, transported and ravished me. . . . Boys and girls tumbling in the street, and playing, were moving jewels. I knew not that they were born or should die. But all things abided eternally as they were in their proper places. Eternity was manifest in the light of day. . . . (Traherne)

William James, America's foremost psychologist, repeatedly stressed that "our normal waking consciousness is but one special type of consciousness, while all about it parted from it by the filmiest of screens there lie potential forms of consciousness entirely different." It is as if our everyday awareness were but an insignificant island, surrounded by a vast ocean of unsuspected and uncharted consciousness, whose waves beat continuously upon the barrier reefs of our normal awareness, until, quite spontaneously, they may break through, flooding our island awareness with knowledge of a vast, largely unexplored, but intensely real domain of new-world consciousness.

Now came a period of rapture so intense that the universe stood still, as if amazed at the unutterable majesty of the spectacle. Only one in all the infinite universe! The All-loving, the Perfect One. . . . In that same wonderful moment of what might be called supernal bliss, came illumination. I saw with intense inward vision the atoms or molecules, of which seemingly the universe is composed—I know not whether material or spiritual—rearranging themselves, as the cosmos (in its continuous, everlasting life) passes from order to order. What joy when I saw there was no break in the chain—not a link left out—everything in its place and time. Worlds, systems, all blended into one harmonious whole. (R. M. Bucke)

The most fascinating aspect of such awesome and illuminating experiences—and the aspect to which we will be devoting much attention—is that the individual comes to feel, beyond any shadow of a doubt, that he or she is fundamentally one with the entire universe, with all worlds, high or low, sacred or profane. The *sense of identity* expands far beyond the narrow confines of the mind and body and embraces the entire cosmos. For just this reason R. M. Bucke referred to this state of awareness as "cosmic consciousness." The Muslim calls it the "Supreme Identity," supreme because it is an identity with the All. We will generally refer to it as "unity consciousness"—a loving embrace with the universe as a whole.

> The streets were mine, the temple was mine, the people were mine. The skies were mine, and so were the sun and moon and stars, and all the world was mine, and I the only spectator and enjoyer of it. I knew no churlish proprieties, nor bounds, nor divisions; but all proprieties and divisions were mine; all treasures and the possessors of them. So that with much ado I was corrupted, and made to learn the dirty devices of this world, which I now unlearn, and become, as it were, a little child again that I may enter into the kingdom of God. (Traherne)

So widespread is this experience of the supreme identity that it has, along with the doctrines that purport to explain it, earned the name "The Perennial Philosophy." There is much evidence that this type of experience or knowledge is central to every major religion—Hinduism, Buddhism, Taoism, Christianity, Islam, and Judaism—so that we can justifiably speak of the "transcendent unity of religions" and the unanimity of primordial truth.

The theme of this book is that this type of awareness, this unity consciousness or supreme identity, is the nature and condition of all sentient beings; but that we progressively limit our world and turn from our true nature in order to embrace boundaries. Our originally pure and nondual consciousness then functions on varied levels, with different identities and different boundaries. These different levels are basically the many ways we can and do answer the question, "Who am I?"

"Who am I?" The query has probably tormented humankind since the dawn of civilization, and remains today one of the most vexing of all human questions. Answers have been offered which range from the sacred to the profane, the complex to the simple, the scientific to the romantic, the political to the individual. But instead of examining the multitude of answers to this question, let's look instead at a very specific and basic process which occurs when a person asks, and then answers, the question "Who am I? What is my real self? What is my fundamental identity?"

When someone asks, "Who are you?" and you proceed to give a reasonable, honest, and more or less detailed answer, what, in fact, are you doing? What goes on in your head as you do this? In one sense you are describing your self as you have come to know it, including in your description most of the pertinent facts, both good and bad, worthy and worthless, scientific and poetic, philosophic and religious, that you understand as fundamental to your identity. You might, for example, think that "I am a unique person, a being endowed with certain potentials; I am kind but sometimes cruel, loving but sometimes hostile; I am a father and lawyer, I enjoy fishing and basketball. . . . "And so your list of feelings and thoughts might proceed.

Yet there is an even more basic process underlying the whole procedure of establishing an identity. Something very simple happens when you answer the question, "Who are you?" When you are describing or explaining or even just inwardly feeling your "self," what you are actually doing, whether you know it or not, is drawing a mental line or boundary across the whole field of your experience, and everything on the *inside* of that boundary you are feeling or calling your "self," while everything *outside* that boundary you feel to be "not-self." Your self-identity, in other words, depends entirely upon where you draw that boundary line.

You are a human and not a chair, and you know that because you consciously or unconsciously draw a boundary line between humans and chairs, and are able to recognize your identity with the former. You may be a very tall human instead of a short one, and so you draw a mental line between tallness and shortness, and thus identify yourself as "tall." You come to feel that "I am this and not that" by drawing a boundary line between "this" and "that" and then recognizing your identity with "this" and your nonidentity with "that."

So when you say "my self," you draw a boundary line between what is you and what is not you. When you answer the question, "Who are you?," you simply describe what's on the inside of that line. The so-called identity crisis occurs when you can't decide how or where to draw the line. In short, "Who are you?" means "Where do you draw the boundary?"

All answers to that question, "Who am I?," stem precisely from this basic procedure of drawing a boundary line between self and not-self. Once the general boundary lines have been drawn up, the answers to that question may become very complex—scientific, theological, economic—or they may remain most simple and unarticulated. But any possible answer depends on first drawing the boundary line.

The most interesting thing about this boundary line is that it can and frequently does shift. It can be redrawn. In a sense, the person can re-map her soul and find in it territories she never thought possible, attainable, or even desirable. As we have seen, the most radical re-mapping or shifting of the boundary line occurs in experiences of the supreme identity, for here the person expands her self-identity boundary to include the entire universe. We might even say that she loses the boundary line altogether, for when she is identified with the "one harmonious whole" there is no longer any outside or inside, and so nowhere to draw the line.

Throughout this book we will return to and examine the no-boundary awareness known as the supreme identity; but at this point it would be worthwhile to investigate some of the other, more familiar ways in which one can define the boundaries of the soul. There are as many different types of boundary lines as there are individuals who draw them, but all of them fall into a handful of easily recognized classes.

The most common boundary line that individuals draw up or accept as valid is that of the skin-boundary surrounding the total organism. This seems to be a universally accepted self/not-self boundary line. Everything on the inside of that skin-boundary is in some sense "me," while everything outside that boundary is "not-me." Something outside the skin-boundary may be "mine," but it's not "me." For example, I recognize "my" car, "my" job, "my" house, "my" family, but they are definitely not directly "me" in the same way all the things inside my skin are "me." The skin-boundary, then, is one of the most fundamentally accepted self/not-self boundaries.

We might think that this skin-boundary is so obvious, so real, and so common that there wouldn't be any other types of boundaries really possible for an individual, save perhaps for those rare occurrences of unity of consciousness on the one hand or the hopelessly psychotic on the other. But in fact there is another extremely common, well-established type of boundary-line drawn by a vast number of individuals. For most people, while they recognize and accept as a matter of course the skin as a self/not-self boundary, draw another and, for them, more significant boundary *within* the total organism itself.

If a boundary line *within* the organism seems strange to you then let me ask, "Do you feel you *are* a body, or do you feel you *have* a body?" Most individuals feel that they *have* a body, as if they owned or possessed it much as they would a car, a house, or any other object. Under these circumstances, the body seems not so much "me" as "mine," and what is "mine," by definition, lies *outside* the self/not-self boundary. The person identifies more basically and intimately with just a facet of his total organism, and this facet, which he feels to be his real self, is known variously as the mind, the psyche, the ego, the personality.

Biologically there is not the least foundation for this dissociation or radical split between the mind and the body, the psyche and the soma, the ego and the flesh, but psychologically it is epidemic. Indeed, the mind-body split and attendant dualism is a fundamental perspective of Western civilization. Notice even here that I must use the word "*psychology*" for the study of overall human behavior. The word itself reflects the prejudice that the human being is basically a mind and not a body. Even St. Francis referred to his body as "poor brother ass," and most of us do indeed feel that we just sort of ride around on our bodies like we would on a donkey or an ass.

This boundary line between the mind and the body is certainly a strange one, not at all present at birth. But as an individual begins to grow in years, and begins to draw up and fortify his self/not-self boundary, he looks upon the body with mixed emotions. Should he directly include it within the boundary of his self, or is it to be viewed as foreign territory? Where is he to draw the line? On the one hand, the body is the source of much pleasure throughout life, from the ecstasies of erotic love to the subtleties of fine foods and mellowness of sunsets taken in by the body's senses. But on the other hand, the body houses the specter of crippling pain, debilitating diseases, and the tortures of cancer. For a child, the body is the only source of pleasure, and yet it is the first source of pain and conflict with the parents. And on top of that, the body seems to be manufacturing waste products that, for reasons totally mystifying to the child, are a constant source of alarm and anxiety for the parents. Bed-wetting, bowel movements, nose-blowing—what an incredible fuss! And it's all tied up with this—the body. Where to draw the line is going to be tough.

But by the time the individual has matured, he has generally kissed poor brother ass good-bye. As the self/not-self boundary is finalized, brother ass is definitely on the other side of the fence. The body becomes foreign territory, almost (but never quite) as foreign as the external world itself. The boundary is drawn between the mind and the body, and the person identifies squarely with the former. He even comes to feel that he lives in his head, as if he were a miniature person in his skull, giving directions and commands to his body, which may or may not obey.

In short, what the individual feels to be his self-identity *does not* directly encompass the organism-as-a-whole, but only a facet of that organism, namely, his ego. That is to say, he identifies with a more or less accurate mental *self-image,* along with the intellectual and emotional processes associated with that self-image. Since he won't concretely identify with the total organism, the most he will allow is a picture or image of the total organism. Thus he feels he is an "ego," and that his body just dangles along under him. So we see here another major type of boundary line, one which establishes the person's identity as being primarily with the ego, the self-image.

As we can see, this self/not-self boundary line can be quite a flexible item. So it won't surprise us to find that even within the ego or mind—I am using these terms very loosely for the moment—yet another type of boundary line can be erected. For various reasons, some of which we will discuss later, the individual can even refuse to admit that some of the facets of her own psyche are *hers.* In psychological jargon, she alienates them, or represses them, or splits them off, or projects them. The point is that she narrows her self/not-self boundary to only certain parts of her egoic tendencies. This narrowed self-image we will be calling the persona, and its meaning will become more obvious as we proceed. But as the individual identifies with only facets of her psyche (the persona), the rest of her psyche is then actually felt to be "not-self," foreign territory, alien, scary. She re-maps her soul so as to deny and try to exclude from consciousness the unwanted aspects of herself (these unwanted aspects we call "shadow"). To a greater or lesser extent, the person becomes "out of her mind." This, quite obviously, is another major and general type of boundary line.

At this point we are not trying to decide which of these types of self-maps is "right," "correct," or "true." We are simply noting, in an impartial fashion, that there are indeed several major types of the self/not-self boundary line. And since we are approaching this topic in a non-judgmental way, we can at least mention one other type of boundary line that is today receiving much attention, namely, the boundary associated with so-called transpersonal phenomena.

"Transpersonal" means that some sort of process is occurring in the individual that, in a sense, goes *beyond* the individual. The simplest instance of this is extrasensory perception, or ESP. Parapsychologists recognize several forms of ESP: telepathy, clairvoyance, precognition, retrocognition. We might also include out-of-body experiences, experiences of a transpersonal self or witness, peak experiences, and so on. What all of these events have in common is an expansion of the self/not-self boundary beyond the skin-boundary of the organism. Although the transpersonal experiences are somewhat similar to unity consciousness, the two should not be confused. In unity consciousness the person's identity is with the All, with absolutely everything. In transpersonal experiences, the person's identity doesn't quite expand to the Whole, but it does expand or at least extend beyond the skin-boundary of the organism. He's not identified with the All, but neither is his identity confined solely to the organism. Whatever one may think of transpersonal experiences (we will discuss many of them in detail later in this book), the evidence that at least some forms of them do exist is overwhelming. Thus, we can safely conclude that these phenomena represent yet another class of self-boundary lines.

The point of this discussion of self/not-self boundaries is that there are not just one but many *levels of identity* available to an individual. These levels of identity are not theoretical postulates but observable realities—you can verify them in and for yourself. As regards these different levels, it's almost as if that familiar yet ultimately mysterious phenomenon we call consciousness were a spectrum, a rainbow-like affair composed of numerous bands or levels of self-identity. Notice that we have briefly outlined five classes or levels of identity. There are certainly variations on these five major levels, and the levels themselves can be extensively subdivided, but these five levels appear to be basic aspects of human consciousness.

Let us take these major levels of identity and arrange them in some sort of order. This spectrum-like arrangement is represented in figure 1, which shows the self/not-self boundary line and the major levels of identity we discussed. Each different level results from the different "places" people can and do draw this boundary. Notice that the boundary line starts to break up toward the bottom of the spectrum (fig. 1), in the area we are calling transpersonal, and that it disappears entirely at the level of unity consciousness, because at that ultimate level self and not-self become "one harmonious whole."

It's obvious that each successive level of the spectrum represents a type of narrowing or restricting of what the individual feels to be his "self," his true identity, his answer to the question, "Who are you?" At the base of the spectrum, the person feels that he is one with the universe, that his real self is not just his organism but all of creation. At the next level of the spectrum (or "moving up" the spectrum), the individual feels that he is not one with the All but rather one with just his total organism. His sense of identity has shifted and narrowed from the uni-

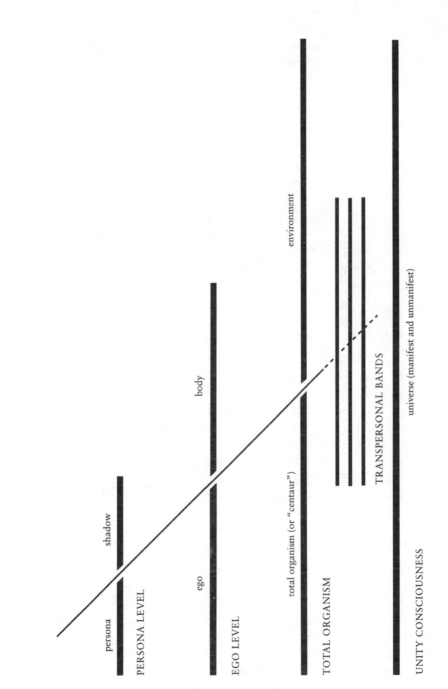

FIGURE 1. The Spectrum of Consciousness

verse as a whole to a facet of the universe, namely, his own organism. At the next level, his self-identity is narrowed once again, for now he identifies mainly with his mind or ego, which is only a facet of his total organism. And on the final level of the spectrum, he can even narrow his identity to facets of his mind, alienating and repressing the shadow or unwanted aspects of his psyche. He identifies with only a part of his psyche, a part we are calling the persona.

Thus, from the universe to a facet of the universe called "the organism"; from the organism to a facet of the organism called "the ego"; from the ego to a facet of the ego called "the persona"—such are some of the major bands of the spectrum of consciousness. With each successive level of the spectrum, there are more and more aspects of the universe which appear to be *external* to the person's "self." Thus, at the level of the total organism, the environment appears outside the self-boundary, foreign, external, not-self. But on the level of the persona, the individual's environment *and* his body *and* aspects of his own psyche appear external, foreign, not-self.

The different levels of the spectrum represent differences not only in self-identity, important as that is, but also in those characteristics which are directly or indirectly bound up with self-identity. Think, for example, of the common problem of "self-conflict." Obviously, since there are different levels of self, there are different levels of self-conflict as well. The reason is that at each level of the spectrum, the boundary line of a person's self is drawn up in a different fashion. But a *boundary line,* as any military expert will tell you, is also a potential *battle line,* for a boundary line marks off the territory of two opposed and potentially warring camps. Thus, for example, a person on the level of the total organism will find the potential enemy is her environment—for it appears foreign, external, and therefore threatening to her life and well-being. But a person on the ego level finds that not only her environment but also her own body are foreign territory, the same foreign territory, and thus the nature of her conflicts and upsets is dramatically different. She has shifted the boundary line of her self, and therefore shifted the battle line of her conflicts and personal wars. And in this case, her body has gone over to the enemy.

This battle line can become acutely prominent on the persona level, for here the individual has drawn the boundary line between facets of her own psyche, and thus the battle line is now between the individual as persona versus her environment *and* her body *and* aspects of her own mind.

The point is that as an individual draws up the boundaries of her soul, she establishes at the same time the battles of her soul. The boundaries of an individual's identity mark off what aspects are to be considered "not-self." So at each level of the spectrum, different aspects of the world appear to be not-self, alien, and foreign. Each level sees different processes of the universe as *strangers* to it. And since, as Freud once remarked, every stranger seems an enemy, every level is potentially engaged in different conflicts with various enemies. Every boundary line, remember, is also a battle line—and the enemy on each level is different. In psychological jargon, different "symptoms" originate from different levels.

The fact that different levels of the spectrum possess different characteristics, symptoms, and potentials, brings us to one of the most interesting points of this view. There is today an incredibly vast and growing interest in all sorts of schools and techniques dealing with various aspects of consciousness. People are flocking to psychotherapy, Jungian analysis, mysticism, Psychosynthesis, Zen, Transactional Analysis, Rolfing, Hinduism, Bioenergetics, psychoanalysis, yoga, and Gestalt. What these schools have in common is that, in one way or another, they are all trying to effect changes in a person's consciousness. But there the similarity ends.

The individual sincerely interested in increasing his self-knowledge is faced with such a bewildering variety of psychological and religious systems that he hardly knows where to begin, whom to believe. Even if he carefully studies all the major schools of psychology and religion, he is apt to come out just as confused as when he went in, for these various schools, taken as a whole, definitely contradict one another. For example, in Zen Buddhism one is told to forget, or transcend, or see through one's ego; but in psychoanalysis, one is helped to strengthen, fortify, and entrench one's ego. Which is right? This is a very real problem, for the interested layperson as well as for the professional therapist. So many different and conflicting schools, all aimed at understanding the very same person. Or are they?

That is, are they all aimed at the *same level* of a person's consciousness? Or is it rather that these different approaches are actually approaches to different levels of a person's self? Could it be that these different approaches, far from being conflicting or contradictory, actually reflect the very real differences in the various levels of the spectrum of consciousness? And could it be that these different approaches are *all* more or less correct when working with their own major level?

If this is true, it allows us to introduce a great deal of order and coherence into this otherwise maddeningly complex field. It would become apparent that all these different schools of psychology and religion do not so much represent contradictory approaches to individuals and their problems, but rather complementary approaches to different levels of the individual. With this understanding, the vast field of psychology and religion breaks down into five or six manageable groups, and it becomes obvious that each of these groups is aiming predominantly at one of the major bands of the spectrum.

Thus, to give just a few very brief and general examples, the aim of psychoanalysis and most forms of conventional psychotherapy is to heal the radical split between the conscious and unconscious aspects of the psyche so that a person is put in touch with "all of his mind." These therapies aim at reuniting the persona and shadow so as to create a strong and healthy ego, which is to say, an accurate and acceptable self-image. In other words, they are all oriented toward the ego level. They seek to help an individual living as persona to re-map the self as ego.

Beyond this, however, the aim of most so-called humanistic therapies is to heal the split between the ego itself and the body, to reunite the psyche and soma so as to reveal the total organism. This is why humanistic psychology—called the Third Force (the other two major forces in psychology being psychoanalysis and behaviorism)—is also referred to as the human potential movement. In extending the person's identity from just the mind or ego to the entire organism-as-a-whole, the vast potentials of the total organism are liberated and put at the individual's disposal.

Going deeper still, we find the aim of such disciplines as Zen Buddhism or Vedanta Hinduism is to heal the split between the total organism and the environment to reveal an identity, a supreme identity, with the entire universe. They are aiming, in other words, for the level of unity consciousness. But let us not forget that between the level of unity consciousness and the level of the total organism there are the transpersonal bands of the spectrum. The therapies addressing this level are deeply concerned with those processes in the person which are actually "supra-individual," or "collective," or "transpersonal." Some of them even refer to a "transpersonal self," and while this transpersonal self is not identical with the All (that would be unity consciousness), it nevertheless transcends the boundaries of the individual organism. Among the therapies aiming at this level are Psychosynthesis, Jungian analysis, various preliminary yoga practices, Transcendental Meditation techniques, and so on.

All of this is of course a very simplified version of things, but it does point out the general fashion in which most of the major schools of psychology, psychotherapy, and religion are simply addressing the different major levels of the spectrum. Some of these correspondences are shown in figure 2, where the major schools of "therapy" are listed beside the level of the spectrum toward which they fundamentally aim. I should mention that because, like any spectrum, these levels shade into one another quite a bit, no absolutely distinct and separate classification of the levels or the therapies addressing those levels is possible. Further, when I "classify" a therapy on the basis of the level of the spectrum it addresses, that means the deepest level which that therapy recognizes, either explicitly or implicitly. Generally speaking, you will find that a therapy of any given level will recognize and accept the potential existence of all of the levels above its own, but deny the existence of all those beneath it.

As a person (layperson or therapist) gains familiarity with the spectrum—its various levels with their different potentials and different problems—she will be better able to orient herself (or her client) in the journey for self-understanding and self-growth. She may be able to recognize more readily from which levels the present problems or conflicts stem, and thus apply to any given conflict the appropriate "therapeutic" process for that level. She may also come to recognize which potentials and levels she wishes to contact, as well as the procedures best suited to facilitate this growth.

Growth fundamentally means an enlarging and expanding of one's horizons, a growth of one's boundaries, outwardly in perspective and inwardly in depth. But that is precisely the definition of *descending* the spectrum. (Or "ascending" it, depending upon which angle you prefer. I will in this book use "descending" simply because it better matches fig. 1.) When a person descends a level of the spectrum he has in effect re-mapped his soul to enlarge its territory. Growth is reapportionment; re-zoning; re-mapping; an acknowledgement, and then enrichment, of ever deeper and more encompassing levels of one's own self.

In the next three chapters we will be exploring some of the facets of the ultimate mystery called unity consciousness, feeling our way into it, edging about it; sneaking up on it, only to have it sneak up on us from behind. Besides giving us some sort of feel for unity consciousness, this

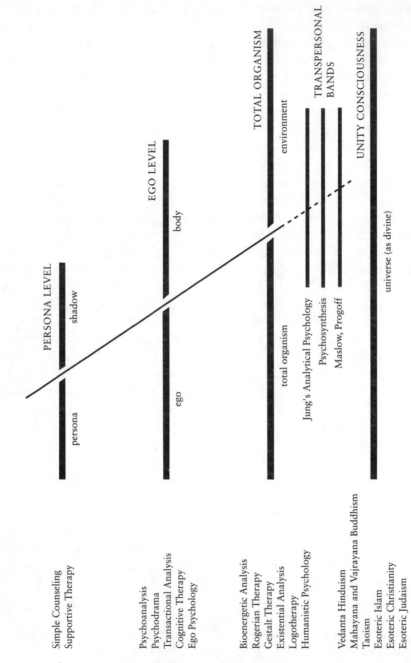

FIGURE 2. Therapies and Levels of the Spectrum

exploration will equip us with many of the necessary tools to understand the whole field of what is today called "transpersonal psychology," "noetics," or "consciousness research." We will explore the world as it appears without limits and boundaries; the present moment as it appears without the boundaries of past and future; and awareness as it appears without the limits of inside and outside.

We will then devote a chapter to explaining the growth of all the other levels of the spectrum: the level of the total organism, the level of ego, and the level of persona. Then, with this basic understanding behind us, we will begin the descent of the spectrum of consciousness; an experiential exploration of the various levels and the major "therapies" used to contact them; ending up, where we began, with the level of unity consciousness. This is only appropriate, for—as we will see—this is the only level that in all truth we have never been without.

2

Half of It

HAVE YOU EVER WONDERED why life comes in opposites? Why everything you value is one of a pair of opposites? Why all decisions are between opposites? Why all desires are based on opposites?

Notice that all spatial and directional dimensions are opposites: up vs. down, inside vs. outside, high vs. low, long vs. short, North vs. South, big vs. small, here vs. there, top vs. bottom, left vs. right. And notice that all things we consider serious and important are one pole of a pair of opposites: good vs. evil, life vs. death, pleasure vs. pain, God vs. Satan, freedom vs. bondage.

So also, our social and esthetic values are always put in terms of opposites: success vs. failure, beautiful vs. ugly, strong vs. weak, intelligent vs. stupid. Even our highest abstractions rest on opposites. Logic, for instance, is concerned with the true vs. the false; epistemology, with appearance vs. reality; ontology, with being vs. non-being. Our world seems to be a massive collection of opposites.

This fact is so commonplace as to hardly need mentioning, but the more one ponders it the more it is strikingly peculiar. For nature, it seems, knows nothing of this world of opposites in which people live. Nature doesn't grow true frogs and false frogs, nor moral trees and immoral trees, nor right oceans and wrong oceans. There is no trace in nature of ethical mountains and unethical mountains. Nor are there even such things as beautiful species and ugly species—at least not to Nature, for it is pleased to produce all kinds. Thoreau said Nature never apologizes, and apparently it's because Nature doesn't know the opposites of right and wrong and thus doesn't recognize what humans imagine to be "errors."

It is certainly true that some of the things which we call "opposites" appear to exist in Nature. There are, for instance, big frogs and small frogs, large trees and small trees, ripe oranges and unripe oranges. But it isn't a problem for them, it doesn't throw them into paroxysms of anxiety. There might even be smart bears and dumb bears, but it doesn't seem to concern them very much. You just don't find inferiority complexes in bears.

Likewise, there is life and death in the world of nature, but again it doesn't seem to hold the terrifying dimensions ascribed to it in the world of humans. A very old cat isn't swept with torrents of terror over its impending death. It just calmly walks out to the woods, curls up under a tree, and dies. A terminally ill robin perches comfortably on the limb of a willow, and stares into the sunset. When finally it can see the light no more, it closes its eyes for the last time and drops gently to the ground. How different from the way humans face death:

> Do not go gentle into that good night
> Rage, rage against the dying of the light.

While pain and pleasure do appear in the world of nature, they are not problems to worry over. When a dog is in pain, it yelps. When not, it just doesn't worry about it. It doesn't dread future pain nor regret past pain. It seems to be a very simple and natural affair.

We say all that is true because, put simply, Nature is dumb. But that won't quite do for a reason. We are just starting to realize that Nature is much smarter than we would like to think. The great biochemist Albert Szent-Gyorgyi gives a whimsical example:

> [When I joined the Institute for Advanced Study in Princeton] I did this in the hope that by rubbing elbows with those great atomic physicists and mathematicians I would learn something about living matters. But as soon as I revealed that in any living system there are more than two electrons, the physicists would not speak to me. With all their computers they could not say what the third electron might do. The remarkable thing is that it knows exactly what to do. So that little electron knows something that all the wise men of Princeton don't, and this can only be something very simple.

I am afraid that Nature is not only smarter than we think, Nature is smarter than we can think. Nature, after all, also produced the human brain, which we flatter ourselves to be one of the most intelligent instruments in the cosmos. And can a total idiot fashion a genuine masterpiece?

According to the Book of Genesis, one of the first tasks given to Adam was to name the animals and plants existing in nature. For nature doesn't come ready-labeled with name tags, and it would be a great convenience if we could classify and name all the various aspects of the natural world. Adam, in other words, was charged with sorting out the complexity of nature's forms and processes and assigning names to them. "These animals look like one another and they don't resemble those animals at all, so let's call this group 'lions' and that group 'bears.' Let's see, you can eat this group of things but not that group. Let's call this group 'grapes' and that group 'rocks.' "

But Adam's real task was not so much thinking up names for the animals and plants, laborious as that undoubtedly was. Rather, the crucial part of his job was the sorting-out process itself. For, unless there were only one of each animal, which is unlikely, Adam had to group together those animals which were similar and learn to mentally differentiate them from dissimilar ones. He had to learn to draw a mental boundary line between the various groups of animals, because only after he did this could he fully recognize, and therefore name, the different beasts. In other words, the great task Adam initiated was the construction of mental or symbolic dividing lines. Adam was the first to delineate nature, to mentally divide it up, mark it off, diagram it. Adam was the first great mapmaker. Adam drew boundaries.

So successful was this mapping of nature that, to this day, our lives are largely spent in drawing boundaries. Every decision we make, our every action, our every word is based on the construction, conscious or unconscious, of boundaries. I am not now referring to just a self-identity boundary—important as that certainly is—but to all boundaries in the broadest sense. To make a decision means to draw a boundary line between what to choose and what not to choose. To desire something means to draw a boundary line between pleasurable and painful things and then move toward the former. To maintain an idea means to draw a boundary line between concepts felt to be true and concepts felt not to be true. To receive an education is to learn where and how to draw boundaries and then what to do with the bounded aspects. To maintain a judicial system is to draw a boundary line between those who fit society's rules and those who don't. To fight a war is to draw a boundary line between those who are for us and those who are against us. To study ethics is to learn how to draw a boundary line disclosing good and evil. To pursue Western medicine is to draw with greater clarity a boundary between sickness and health. Quite obviously, from minor incidents to major crises, from small decisions to big deals, from mild preferences to flaming passions, our lives are a process of drawing boundaries.

The peculiar thing about a boundary is that, however complex and rarefied it might be, it actually marks off nothing but an inside vs. an outside. For example, we can draw the very simplest form of a boundary line as a circle, and see that it discloses an inside versus an outside:

But notice that the opposites of inside vs. outside didn't exist in themselves until we drew the boundary of the circle. It is the boundary line itself, in other words, which creates a pair of opposites. In short, to draw boundaries is to manufacture opposites. Thus we can start to see that the reason we live in a world of opposites is precisely because life as we know it is a process of drawing boundaries.

And the world of opposites is a world of conflict, as Adam himself would soon discover. Adam must have been fascinated with the power generated by drawing boundary lines and invoking names. Imagine: a simple sound such as "sky" could represent the whole immensity and vastness of the blue heavens, which were, by the power of boundary lines, recognized to be different from the earth, from water, from fire. So instead of handling and manipulating real objects, Adam could manipulate in his head these magic names which stood for the objects themselves. Before the invention of boundaries and names, for example, if Adam wanted to tell Eve that he thought she was as dumb as a jackass, he had to grab Eve and then wander around until he also found a jackass, and then point to the jackass, then point to Eve, then jump up and down and grunt and make stupid faces. But now, through the magic of words, Adam could just look up and say, "Good heavens, my dear, you are quite as dumb as a jackass." Eve, who by the way was really much wiser than Adam, usually held her tongue. That is, she declined to reciprocate with word magic, for she knew in her heart that words were a two-edged sword, and that he who lives by the sword, perishes by the sword.

In the meantime, the results of Adam's endeavors were spectacular, powerful, magical, and he understandably started to get a little cocky. He started extending boundaries into, and thus gaining knowledge over, places that were better left uncharted. This cocky behavior culminated at the Tree of Knowledge, which was really the tree of the opposites of good and evil. And when Adam recognized the difference between the opposites of good and evil, that is, when he drew a fatal boundary, his world fell apart. When Adam sinned, the entire world of opposites, which he himself had helped to create, returned to plague him. Pain vs. pleasure, good vs. evil, life vs. death, toil vs. play—the whole array of conflicting opposites swept down on humankind.

The exasperating fact which Adam learned was that every boundary line is also a potential battle line, so that just to draw a boundary is to prepare oneself for conflict. Specifically, the conflict of the war of opposites, the agonizing fight of life against death, pleasure against pain, good against evil. What Adam learned—and learned too late—is that "Where to draw the line?" really means, "Where the battle is to take place."

The simple fact is that we live in a world of conflict and opposites because we live in a world of boundaries. Since every boundary line is also a battle line, here is the human predicament: the firmer one's boundaries, the more entrenched are one's battles. The more I hold onto pleasure, the more I necessarily fear pain. The more I pursue goodness, the more I am obsessed with evil. The more I seek success, the more I must dread failure. The harder I cling to life, the more terrifying death becomes. The more I value anything, the more obsessed I become with its loss. Most of our problems, in other words, are problems of boundaries and the opposites they create.

Now our habitual way of trying to solve these problems is to attempt to eradicate one of the opposites. We handle the problem of good vs. evil by trying to exterminate evil. We handle the problem of life vs. death by trying to hide death under symbolic immortalities. In philosophy we handle conceptual opposites by dismissing one of the poles or trying to reduce it to the other. The materialist tries to reduce mind to matter, while the idealist tries to reduce matter to mind. The monists try to reduce plurality to unity, the pluralists try to explain unity as plurality.

The point is that we always tend to treat the boundary as *real* and then manipulate the opposites created by the boundary. We never seem to question the existence of the boundary itself. Because we believe the boundary to be real, we staunchly imagine that the opposites are irreconcilable, separate, forever set apart. "East is East and West is West and never the twain shall meet." God and Satan, life and death, good and evil, love and hate, self and other—these are as different, we say, as night and day.

Thus we suppose that life would be perfectly enjoyable if we could only eradicate all the negative and unwanted poles of the pairs of opposites. If we could vanquish pain, evil, death, suffering, sickness, so that goodness, life, joy, and health would abound—that, indeed, would be the good life, and in fact, that is precisely many people's idea of Heaven. Heaven has come to mean, not a transcendence of all opposites, but the place where all the positive halves of the pairs of opposites are accumulated, while Hell is the place where are massed all the negative halves: pain, suffering, torment, anxiety, sickness.

This goal of separating the opposites and then clinging to or pursuing the positive halves seems to be a distinguishing characteristic of progressive Western civilization—its religion, science, medicine, industry. Progress, after all, is simply progress *toward* the positive and *away* from the negative. Yet, despite the obvious comforts of medicine and agriculture, there is not the least bit of evidence to suggest that, after centuries of accentuating positives and trying to eliminate negatives, humanity is any happier, more content, or more at peace with itself. In fact, the available evidence suggests just the contrary: today is the "age of anxiety," of "future shock," of epidemic frustration and alienation, of boredom in the midst of wealth and meaninglessness in the midst of plenty.

It seems that "progress" and unhappiness might well be flip sides of the same restless coin. For the very urge to *progress* implies a discontent with the *present* state of affairs, so that the more I seek progress the more acutely I feel discontent. In blindly pursuing progress, our civilization has, in effect, institutionalized frustration. For in seeking to accentuate the positive and eliminate the negative, we have forgotten entirely that the positive is defined only in terms of the negative. The opposites might indeed be as different as night and day, but the essential point is that without night we would not even be able to recognize something called day. To destroy the negative is, at the same time, to destroy all possibility of enjoying the positive. Thus, the more we succeed in this adventure of progress, the more we actually fail, and hence the more acute becomes our sense of total frustration.

The root of the whole difficulty is our tendency to view the opposites as irreconcilable, as totally set apart and divorced from one another.

Even the simplest of opposites, such as buying versus selling, are viewed as two different and separate events. Now it is true that buying and selling are in some sense different, but they are also—and this is the point—completely *inseparable*. Any time you buy something, someone else has, in the same action, sold something. In other words, buying and selling are simply *two* ends of *one* event, namely, the single business transaction itself. And while the two ends of the transaction are "different," the single event which they represent is one and the same.

In just the same way, all of the opposites share an implicit identity. That is, however vividly the differences between these opposites may strike us, they nevertheless remain completely inseparable and mutually interdependent, and for the simple reason that the one could not exist without the other. Looked at in this way, there is obviously no inside without an outside, no up without down, no win without loss, no pleasure without pain, no life without death. Says the old Chinese sage Lao Tzu:

> Is there a difference between yes and no?
> Is there a difference between good and evil?
> Must I fear what others fear? What nonsense!
> Having and not having arise together
> Difficult and easy complement each other
> Long and short contrast each other
> High and low rest upon each other
> Front and back follow one another.

Chuang Tzu elaborates:

> Thus, those who say that they would have right without its correlate, wrong; or good government without its correlate, misrule, do not apprehend the great principles of the universe, nor the nature of all creation. One might as well talk of the existence of Heaven without that of Earth, or of the negative principle without the positive, which is clearly impossible. Yet people keep on discussing it without stop; such people must be either fools or knaves.

The inner unity of opposites is hardly an idea confined to mystics, Eastern or Western. If we look to modern-day physics, the field in which the Western intellect has made its greatest advances, what we find is another version of reality as a union of opposites. In relativity theory, for example, the old opposites of rest vs. motion have become totally indistinguishable, that is, "each is both." An object which appears at rest for one observer is, at the same time, in motion for a different observer. Likewise, the split between wave and particle vanishes into "wavicles," and the contrast of structure vs. function evaporates. Even the age-old separation of mass from energy has fallen to Einstein's $E = mc^2$, and these ancient "opposites" are not viewed as merely two aspects of one reality, a reality to which Hiroshima so violently bore witness.

Likewise, such opposites as subject vs. object and time vs. space are now seen as being so mutually interdependent that they form an interwoven continuum, a single unified pattern. What we call "subject" and "object" are, like buying and selling, just two different ways of approaching one single process. And because the same holds true for time and space, we can no longer speak of an object being located in space or happening in time, but only of a spacetime occurrence. Modern physics, in short, proclaims that reality can only be considered a union of opposites. In the words of biophysicist Ludwig von Bertalanffy:

> If what has been said is true, reality is what Nicholas of Cusa called the *coincidentia oppositorum*. Discursive thinking always represents only one aspect of ultimate reality, called God in Cusa's terminology; it can never exhaust its infinite manifoldness. Hence ultimate reality is a unity of opposites.

From the viewpoint of *coincidentia oppositorum*—"the coincidence of opposites"—what we thought were totally separate and irreconcilable opposites turn out to be, in von Bertalanffy's phrase, "complimentary aspects of one and the same reality."

It is for all these reasons that Alfred North Whitehead, one of the most influential philosophers of this century, set forth his philosophy of "organism" and "vibratory existence," which suggests that all the "ultimate elements are in their essence vibratory." That is, all the things and events we usually consider are irreconcilable, such as cause and effect, past and future, subject and object, are actually just like the crest and trough of a single wave, a single vibration. For a wave, although itself a single event, only expresses itself through the opposites of crest and trough, high point and low point. For that very reason, the reality is not found in the crest nor the trough alone, but in their unity (try to imagine a wave with crests but no troughs). Obviously, there's no such thing as a crest without a trough, a high point without a low point. Crest and trough—indeed all opposites—are inseparable aspects of one underlying activity. Thus, as Whitehead puts it, each element of the universe is "a vibratory ebb and flow of an underlying energy or activity."

Nowhere is this inner unity of opposites set forth more clearly than in the Gestalt theory of perception. According to Gestalt, we are never aware of any object or event or figure save in relation to a contrasting background. For example, something we call "light" is really a light figure standing out against a dark background. When I look up to the heavens on a dark night and perceive the brilliance of a bright star, what I am really seeing—what my eye actually "takes in"—is not the separate star, but the entire field or Gestalt of "bright star *plus* dark background." However drastic the contrast between the bright star and its background of darkness, the point is that without the one I could never perceive the other. "Light" and "dark" are thus two correlative aspects of one single sensory Gestalt. Likewise, I cannot perceive motion except in relation to rest, nor effort without ease, nor complexity without simplicity, nor attraction without repulsion.

In the same way, I am never aware of pleasure except in relation to pain. I might indeed be feeling very comfortable and pleasurable at this moment, but I would never be able to *realize* that were it not for the background existence of discomfort and pain. This is why pleasure and pain always seem to alternate, for it is only in their mutual contrast and alternation that the existence of each can be recognized. Thus, as much as I like the one and loathe the other, the attempt to isolate them is futile. As Whitehead would say, pleasure and pain are just the inseparable crest and trough of a single wave of awareness, and to try to accentuate the positive crest and eliminate the negative trough is to try to eliminate the wave of awareness itself.

Perhaps we can begin to understand why life, when viewed as a world of separate opposites, is so totally frustrating, and why progress has actually become not a growth but a cancer. In trying to separate the opposites and cling to those we judge positive, such as pleasure without pain, life without death, good without evil, we are really striving after phantoms without the least reality. Might as well strive for a world of crests and no troughs, buyers and no sellers, lefts and no rights, ins and no outs. Thus, as Wittgenstein pointed out, because our goals are not lofty but illusory, our problems are not difficult but nonsensical.

That all opposites—such as mass and energy, subject and object, life and death—are so much each other that they are perfectly inseparable, still strikes most of us as hard to believe. But this is only because we accept as real the *boundary line* between the opposites. It is, recall, the boundaries themselves which create the seeming existence of separate opposites. To put it plainly, to say that "ultimate reality is a unity of opposites" is actually to say that *in ultimate reality there are no boundaries*. Anywhere.

The fact is, we are so bewitched by boundaries, so under the spell of Adam's sin, that we have totally forgotten the actual nature of boundary lines themselves. For boundary lines, of any type, are never found in the real world itself, but only in the imagination of mapmakers. To be sure, there are many kinds of *lines* in the natural world, such as the shoreline situated between continents and the oceans surrounding them. There are, in fact, all sorts of lines and surfaces in nature—outlines of leaves and skins of organisms, skylines and tree lines and lake lines, surfaces of light and shade, and lines setting off all objects from their environment. Obviously those surfaces and lines are actually there, but those lines, such as the shoreline between land and water, don't merely represent a *separation* of land and water, as we generally suppose. As Alan Watts pointed out so often, those so-called "dividing lines" equally represent precisely those places where the land and water *touch* each other. That is, those lines *join* and *unite* just as much as they divide and distinguish. These lines, in other words, aren't boundaries! There is a vast difference between a line and a boundary, as we shall presently see.

The point, then, is that lines join the opposites as well as distinguish them. And that precisely is the essence and function of all real lines and surfaces in nature. They explicitly mark off the opposites while at the same time they implicitly unify them. For example, let's draw the line representing a concave figure, as follows:

But notice immediately that with the very same line I have also created a convex figure. This is what the Taoist sage Lao Tzu meant when he said that all opposites arise simultaneously and mutually. Like concave and convex in this example, they come into existence together.

Further, we cannot say that the line *separates* concave from convex, because there is only one line and it is wholly shared by both. The line, far from separating concave and convex, makes it absolutely impossible for the one to exist without the other. Because of that single line, no matter how we draw a concave, we have also drawn a convex, because the outline of the concave *is* the inline of the convex. Thus, you will never find a concave without a convex, for these, like all opposites, are fated to intimately embrace one another for all time.

The point is that all of the lines we find in nature, or even construct ourselves, do not merely distinguish different opposites, but also bind the two together in an inseparable unity. A line, in other words, is not a boundary. For a line, whether mental, natural, or logical doesn't just divide and separate, it also joins and unites. Boundaries, on the other hand, are pure illusions—they pretend to separate what is not in fact separable. In this sense, the actual world contains lines but no real boundaries.

A real line becomes an illusory boundary when we imagine its two sides to be separated and unrelated; that is, when we acknowledge the outer difference of the two opposites but ignore their inner unity. A line becomes a boundary when we forget that the inside co-exists with the outside. A line becomes a boundary when we imagine that it just separates but doesn't unite at the same time. It is fine to draw lines, provided we do not mistake them for boundaries. It is fine to distinguish pleasure from pain; it is impossible to separate pleasure from pain.

Now we generate the illusions of boundaries in much the same way Adam originally did, for the sins of the fathers have been visited on their sons and daughters. We begin by either following the lines of nature—shorelines, forest lines, sky lines, rock surfaces, skin surfaces, and so on—or by constructing our own mental lines (which are ideas and concepts). By this process we sort out and classify aspects of our world. We learn to recognize the difference between the inside and outside of our classes: between what are rocks and what are not rocks, between what is pleasure and what is not pleasure, between what is tall and what is not tall, between what is good and what is not good. . . .

Already our lines are in danger of becoming boundaries, for we are recognizing explicit differences and forgetting the implicit unity. And this error is facilitated as we proceed to name, to attach a word or symbol to, the inside and outside of the class. For the words we use for the inside of the class, such as "light," "up," "pleasure," are definitely detachable and separate from the words we use for the outside of the class, such as "dark," "down," and "pain."

Thus, we can manipulate the symbols independently of their mandatory opposites. For instance, I can create a sentence which says, "I want

pleasure," and there is no reference in that sentence to pleasure's neces-'
sary opposite, pain. I can separate pleasure and pain in words, in my
thoughts, even though in the real world the one is never found apart
from the other. At this point, the line between pleasure and pain becomes a boundary, and the illusion that the two are separate seems con-
vincing. Not seeing that the opposites are just two different names for
one process, I imagine there are two different processes set against each
other. Commenting on this, L. L. Whyte said, "Thus, the immature
mind, unable to escape its own prejudice . . . is condemned to struggle in
the straitjacket of its dualisms: subject/object, time/space, spirit/matter,
freedom/necessity, free will/law. The truth, which must be single, is ridden with contradiction. Man cannot think where he is, for he has *created
two worlds from one.*"

Our problem, it seems, is that we create a conventional map, complete with boundaries, of the actual territory of nature, which has no
boundaries, and then thoroughly confuse the two. As Korzybski and
the general semanticists have pointed out, our words, symbols, signs,
thoughts and ideas are merely maps of reality, not reality itself, because
"the map is not the territory." The word "water" won't satisfy your
thirst. But we live in the world of maps and words as if it were the real
world. Following in the footsteps of Adam, we have become totally lost
in a world of purely fantasy maps and boundaries. And these illusory
boundaries, with the opposites they create, have become our impas-
sioned battles.

Most of our "problems of living," then, are based on the illusion that
the opposites can and should be separated and isolated from one another. But since all opposites are actually aspects of one underlying reality, this is like trying to totally separate the two ends of a single rubber
band. All you can do is pull harder and harder—until something violently snaps.

Thus we might be able to understand that, in all the mystical traditions the world over, one who sees through the illusion of the opposites
is called "liberated." Because he is "freed from the pairs" of opposites,
he is freed in this life from the fundamentally nonsensical problems and
conflicts involved in the war of opposites. He no longer manipulates
the opposites one against the other in his search for peace, but instead
transcends them both. Not good vs. evil but beyond good and evil. Not
life against death but a center of awareness that transcends both. The
point is not to separate the opposites and make "positive progress," but
rather to unify and harmonize the opposites, both positive and negative,

by discovering a ground which transcends and encompasses them both. And that ground, as we will soon see, is unity consciousness itself. In the meantime, let us note, as does the Hindu scripture *Bhagavad Gita*, that liberation is not freedom from the negative, but freedom from the pairs altogether:

> Content with getting what arrives of itself
>   Passed beyond the pairs, free from envy,
> Not attached to success nor failure,
>   Even acting, he is not bound.
> He is to be recognized as eternally free
>   Who neither loathes nor craves;
> For he that is freed from the pairs,
>   Is easily freed from conflict.

This being "freed from the pairs" is, in Western terms, the discovery of the Kingdom of Heaven on earth, even though the popular evangelists have forgotten it. For Heaven is not, as pop religion would have it, a state of all positives and no negatives, but the state of realizing "no-opposites" or "not-two-ness," at least according to the Gospel of St. Thomas:

> They said to Him: Shall we then, being children,
> enter the Kingdom? Jesus said to them:
> When you make the two one, and
> when you make the inner as the outer
> and the outer as the inner and the above
> as the below, and when
> you make the male and the female into a single one,
> then you shall enter the Kingdom.

This idea of no-opposites and not-two-ness is the essence of Advaita Hinduism (*advaita* means "nondual" or "not-two") and of Mahayana Buddhism. The idea is beautifully expressed in one of the most important Buddhist texts, the *Lankavatara Sutra*:

> False-imagination teaches that such things as light and shade, long and short, black and white are different and are to be discriminated; but they are not independent of each other; they are only different aspects of the same thing, they are terms of rela-

tion, not of reality. Conditions of existence are not of a mutually exclusive character; in essence things are not two but one.

We could multiply these quotes indefinitely, but they would all point to the same thing: ultimate reality is a union of opposites. And since it is expressly the boundaries which we superimpose on reality that slice it up into innumerable pairs of opposites, the claim of all these traditions that reality is freed from the pairs of opposites is a claim that reality is freed from all boundaries. That reality is not-two means that reality is no-boundary.

Thus the solution to the war of the opposites requires the surrendering of all boundaries, and not the progressive juggling of the opposites against each other. The war of opposites is a symptom of a boundary taken to be real, and to cure the symptoms we must go to the root of the matter itself: our illusory boundaries.

But, we ask, what will happen to our drive for progress if we see all opposites are one? Well, with any luck, it will stop—and with it that peculiar discontent that thrives on the illusion that the grass is greener on the other side of the fence. But we should be clear about this. I do not mean that we will cease making advancements of a sort in medicine, agriculture, and technology. We will only cease to harbor the illusion that happiness depends on it. For when we see through the illusions of our boundaries, we will see, here and now, the universe as Adam saw it before the Fall: an organic unity, a harmony of opposites, a melody of positive and negative, delight with the play of our vibratory existence. When the opposites are realized to be one, discord melts into concord, battles become dances, and old enemies become lovers. We are then in a position to make friends with all of our universe, and not just one half of it.

3

No-Boundary Territory

THE ULTIMATE METAPHYSICAL SECRET, if we dare state it so simply, is that there are no boundaries in the universe. Boundaries are illusions, products not of reality but of the way we map and edit reality. And while it is fine to map out the territory, it is fatal to confuse the two.

It's not just that there are no boundaries between the opposites. In a much wider sense, there are no dividing boundaries between any things or events anywhere in the cosmos. And nowhere is the reality of no-boundary seen more clearly than in modern physics, which is all the more remarkable considering that classical physics—associated with such names as Kepler, Galileo, and Newton—was one of the true heirs of Adam the mapmaker and boundary drawer.

When Adam finally passed on, he left humankind his legacy of mapmaking and boundary drawing. And since every boundary carries with it political and technological power, Adam's bounding, classifying, and naming of nature marked the first beginnings of technological power and control over nature. As a matter of fact, Hebrew tradition has it that the fruit of the Tree of Knowledge actually harbored knowledge not of good and evil but of the useful and the useless—that is, technological knowledge. But if every boundary carries technological and political power, it also carries alienation, fragmentation, and conflict—because when you establish a boundary so as to gain control over something, at the same time you separate and alienate yourself from that which you

30

attempt to control. Hence the Fall of Adam into fragmentation, known as original sin.

Yet the boundaries Adam drew were very simple kinds of boundaries. They merely classified, and were useful only in description, definition, naming, and so on. And Adam didn't even make full use of these classifying boundaries. He had hardly gotten around to naming vegetables and fruits when he fumbled the ball and got kicked out of the game.

Generations later, the descendants of Adam finally worked up enough nerve to start fooling around with boundaries again, and more subtle and abstract boundaries at that. In Greece men of brilliant intellectual powers appeared—that is, great mapmakers and boundary drawers. Aristotle, for instance, classified nearly every process and thing in nature with such precision and persuasion that it would take centuries for Europeans just to question the validity of his boundaries.

But no matter how precise and complex your classifications, you can't do very much—scientifically at least—with that type of boundary line except describe and define. You have only a qualitative science, a classifying science. However, once you have laid down your initial boundaries, so that the world appears as a complex of separate things and events, you can then proceed to much more subtle and abstract types of boundaries. And the Greeks, like Pythagoras, did just that.

For what Pythagoras discovered, looking over all the various classes of things and events, from horses to oranges to stars, was that he could perform a brilliant trick on all these different objects. He could, in fact, count them.

If naming seemed magic, counting seemed divine, because while names could magically represent things, numbers could transcend them. For instance, one orange plus one orange equals two oranges, but so does one apple plus one apple equal two apples. The number two refers impartially to any and all groups of two things, and so somehow must transcend them.

Through abstract numbers, humans succeeded in freeing their minds from concrete things. To some extent this was possible through the first type of boundary, through naming, classifying, and noting differences. But numbers increased this power dramatically. For, in a sense, counting was actually a totally new type of boundary. It was a boundary on a boundary, a meta-boundary, and it worked like this:

With the first type of boundary, we draw a dividing line between different things and then recognize them as constituting a group or class, which we then name frogs, cheeses, mountains, or whatnot. This is the

first or basic type of boundary. Once we have drawn our first boundaries, we can then draw a *second* type of boundary on the first type and
then count the things in our classes. If the first boundary gives a class of
things, the second boundary gives a class of classes of things. So, for
example, the number seven refers equally to *all* the groups or classes of
things which have seven members. Seven can refer to seven grapes, seven
days, seven dwarfs, and so on. The number seven, in other words, is a
group of all the groups which have seven members. It is therefore a
class of classes, a boundary on a boundary. Thus with numbers, humans
constructed a new type of boundary, a more abstract and generalized
boundary, a *meta-boundary*. And since boundaries carry political and
technological power, humans had thereby increased their ability to control the natural world.

However, these new and more powerful boundaries brought with
them the potential not only for a more developed technology, but also a
more pervasive alienation and fragmentation. The Greeks succeeded in
introducing, through this new meta-boundary of number, a subtle conflict, a subtle dualism, which has fastened onto Europeans as a vampire
battens on its prey. For abstract numbers, this new meta-boundary, so
transcended the concrete world that humans discovered they were now
living in two worlds—the concrete vs. the abstract, the ideal vs. the real,
the universal vs. the particular. Over the next two thousand years this
dualism would change its form a dozen times, but rarely be uprooted or
harmonized. It became a battle of the rational vs. the romantic, ideas vs.
experience, intellect vs. instinct, law vs. chaos, mind vs. matter. Those
distinctions were all based on appropriate and real lines, but the lines
usually degenerated into boundaries and battles.

This new meta-boundary—that of number, counting, measuring, and
the like—was not really put to use by natural scientists for centuries,
until the time of Galileo and Kepler, around the year 1600. For the
intervening period between the Greeks and the first classical physicists
was occupied by a new force on the European scene—the Church. And
the Church would have none of that measuring or scientifically number-
ing-up of nature. The Church, through the influence of Thomas Acqui-
nas, was closely allied with the logic of Aristotle, and Aristotle's logic,
for all its brilliance, was predominantly one of classifying. Aristotle was
a biologist, and carried on the classifying begun by Adam. He never
really got the full swing of Pythagorean number and measurement. And
so neither did the Church.

But by the seventeenth century, the Church was in decline, and humans began looking carefully at the forms and processes of the natural world. And it was at this time that the genius of Galileo and Kepler entered the drama. The revolutionary thing these physicists accomplished was simply to *measure,* and measurement is just a very sophisticated form of counting. So where Adam and Aristotle drew boundaries, Kepler and Galileo drew meta-boundaries.

But the seventeenth-century scientists didn't just resurrect the meta-boundary of number and measurement and then sophisticate it. They went one step further and introduced (or rather, perfected) an entirely new boundary of their own. Incredible as it seems, they came up with a boundary on the meta-boundary. They invented the meta-meta-boundary, better known as algebra.

Put simply, the first boundary produces a class. The meta-boundary produces a class of classes, called number. The third or meta-meta-boundary produces a class of classes of classes, called the variable. The variable is best known as that which is represented in formulas as x, y, or z. And the variable works like this: just as a number can represent *any thing,* a variable can represent *any number.* Just as five can refer to any five things, x can refer to any number over a given range.

By using algebra, the early scientists could proceed not only to number and measure the elements, but also to search out abstract relations between those measurements, which could be expressed in theories, laws, and principles. And these laws seemed, in some sense, to "govern" or "control" all the things and events marked off with the very first type of boundaries. The early scientists produced laws by the dozens: "For every action there is an equal and opposite reaction." "Force is equal to the mass times the acceleration of the en-forced body." "The amount of work done on a body equals the force times the distance."

This new type of boundary, the meta-meta-boundary, brought new knowledge and, of course, explosive new technological and political power. Europe was rocked with an intellectual revolution the likes of which humankind had never seen. Just imagine: Adam could name the planets; Pythagoras could count them; but Newton could tell you how much they weighed.

Notice, then: this entire process of formulating scientific laws was based on three general types of boundaries, each building on its predecessor and each being more abstract and generalized. First, you draw a classifying boundary, so as to recognize different things and events. Second, you search among your classified elements for ones that can be measured. This meta-boundary allows you to shift quality to quantity, classes to classes of classes, elements to measurements. Third, you search for relationships between your numbers and measurements of the second step until you can invent an algebraic formula embracing them all. This meta-meta-boundary converts measurements to conclusions, numbers to principles. Each step, each new boundary, brings you a more generalized knowledge, and hence more power.

This knowledge, power, and control over nature was, however, bought at a price, for, as always, a boundary is a double-edged sword, and the fruits it slices from nature are necessarily bittersweet. Man had gained control over nature, but only by radically separating himself from it. In the mere span of ten generations, he had for the first time in history awarded himself the dubious honor of being able to blast the entire planet, himself included, to smithereens. The earth's heavens were so choked with fumes that birds were abandoning existence; the lakes so clogged with greasy sludge that some of them would spontaneously catch fire; the oceans so dense with insoluble chemical jello that fish were buoyed to the surface like Styrofoam on mercury; and the rains that fell to the earth in some places would corrode sheet metal.

And yet, during the span of ten generations, a second revolution in science was forming. Nobody guessed, or could have guessed, that this revolution, when it finally culminated around 1925, would signal the surpassing of classical physics—its boundaries, meta-boundaries, and meta-meta-boundaries. The whole world of classical boundaries shattered and fell before the likes of Einstein, Schroedinger, Eddington, deBroglie, Bohr, and Heisenberg.

As you read the accounts of this twentieth-century revolution in science given by these physicists themselves, you can't help being struck by the awesome nature of the intellectual upheaval that occurred in the brief span of a single generation, 1905–1925, dating from Einstein's relativity theory to Heisenberg's uncertainty principle. The classical boundaries and maps of the old physics literally fell apart. In 1925, Whitehead stated, "The progress of science has now reached a turning point. The stable foundations of physics have broken up. . . . The old foundations of scientific thought are becoming unintelligible. Time, space, matter, material, ether, electricity, mechanism, organism, configuration, structure, pattern, function, all require reinterpretation. What is the sense of talking about a mechanical explanation when you do not know what you mean by mechanics?" And Louis deBroglie said, "On the day when quanta, surreptitiously, were introduced the vast and grandiose edifice of classical physics found itself shaken to its very foundations. In the history of the intellectual world there have been few upheavals comparable to this."

To understand why this "quantum revolution" was such a cataclysmic upheaval, remember that by the dawn of the twentieth century, the world of science had enjoyed about fourteen decades of astounding success. The universe was viewed, at least through the eyes of the classical physicists, as a magnificent but inarticulate collection of separate things and events, each perfectly isolated by definite boundaries in space and time. Further, these separate entities—planets, rocks, meteors, apples, peoples—were thought capable of being precisely measured and numbered, a process which in turn eventually yielded scientific laws and principles.

So successful was this procedure that scientists began dreaming that all of nature was governed by these laws. The world was viewed as a giant Newtonian billiard table, where all the separate things in the universe acted like billiard balls, blindly smashing around and occasionally colliding with one another. As scientists began exploring the world of subatomic physics, they naturally assumed that all the old Newtonian laws, or something like them, would apply to the protons, neutrons, and electrons. But they didn't. Not at all, not even a little. The shock was comparable to pulling off your glove one day and finding a lobster claw where you expected your hand.

Worse yet, it wasn't just that these "ultimate realities," like the electrons, didn't fit the old physical laws. These ultimate realities couldn't even be located! As Heisenberg put it, "We can no longer consider 'in themselves' those buildingstones of matter which we originally held to be the last objective reality. This is so because they defy all forms of objective location in space and time." Not only did the subatomic billiard balls not obey established laws, the billiard balls themselves didn't even exist—at least not as separate entities. The atom, in other words, wasn't behaving like a discrete "thing." The old physics had metaphorically viewed the atom as a miniature solar system, with neutrons and protons composing the sun nucleus, and discrete planetary electrons spinning around it. But now the atom began to look more like a nebulous cloud that infinitely shaded into its environment. As Henry Stapp put it, "An elementary particle is not an independently existing unanalyzable entity. It is, in essence, a set of relationships that reach outward to other things." These "atomic things," the ultimate building blocks of all reality, couldn't be located because, in short, they had no boundaries.

Moreover, because these "ultimate realities" of the universe had no definite boundaries, they couldn't be adequately measured. This was extremely disconcerting to the physicists, because their stock-in-trade was the ruler of scientific measurement, numbering, meta-boundaries. The fact that these basic realities could never be totally measured, under any circumstances, was called the Heisenberg uncertainty principle, and it capped the final end of classical physics. Heisenberg himself called it "the dissolution of the rigid frame." The old boundaries had collapsed.

Because the subatomic particles possessed no boundaries, there could be no meta-boundaries, no measurements; and hence also, no precise meta-meta-boundaries, no "laws." To this day there is no law, no meta-meta-map, governing the movements of a single electron, because a single electron doesn't have a boundary in the first place. You can't have a meta-boundary or a meta-meta-boundary if there isn't even a boundary to begin with. Nuclear physicists must now work with probabilities and statistics. This means that they must gather together for their measurements enough atomic elements that the physicists can pretend that the collected group looks like a distinct thing with a make-believe boundary. Then they can construct meta-boundaries and offer up an educated guess as to how the system, as a whole, might behave. But the crucial item is that the physicists now *know* that these boundaries are pretend and make-believe, and that the basic constituents themselves remain no-boundary.

It is now easier to see what went wrong with the old physics. It has been so enraptured with the success of its meta-boundaries and meta-meta-boundaries that it totally forgot the conventional nature of the original boundaries themselves. The meta-boundaries and meta-meta-boundaries were so useful, and carried such political and technological power, that it never dawned on the classical physicists that their *original* boundaries might be false. To put it another way, they developed laws governing separate things, only to discover that separate things don't exist.

The new quantum physicists were forced to recognize the conventional nature of the original boundaries themselves, and for the simple reason that they couldn't find any real ones. Boundaries, instead of being a product of reality, there for all to feel and touch and measure, were finally seen as a product of the way we map and edit reality. Said the physicist Eddington: "We have found that where science has progressed the farthest, the mind has but regained from nature that which the mind has put into nature. We have found a strange footprint on the shores of the unknown. We have devised profound theories, one after another, to account for its origin. At last, we have succeeded in reconstructing the creature that made the footprint. And lo! it is our own."

This is not to say that the real world is a mere product of our imaginations (subjective idealism), only that our boundaries are. This is why Wittgenstein said that, "At the basis of the whole modern view of the world lies the illusion that the so-called laws of nature are the explanations of natural phenomena." For these laws describe not reality but only our boundaries of reality. As Wittgenstein put it, "Laws, like the law of causation, etc., treat of the network [of boundaries] and not of what the network describes."

In short, the quantum physicists discovered that reality could no longer be viewed as a complex of distinct things and boundaries. Rather, what were once thought to be bounded "things" turned out to be interwoven aspects of each other. For some strange reason, every thing and event in the universe seemed to be interconnected with every other thing and event in the universe. The world, the real territory, began to look not like a collection of billiard balls but more like a single, giant, universal field, which Whitehead called the "seamless coat of the universe." These physicists, it seems, succeeded in catching a glimpse of the real world, the territory of no-boundary, the world Adam saw before he drew his fatal boundaries, the world as it is and not as it is classified, bounded, mapped, meta-mapped. Teilhard de Chardin speaks of this seamless coat:

> Considered in its concrete reality, the stuff of the universe cannot divide itself but, as a kind of gigantic atom, it forms in its totality the only real indivisible. . . . The farther and more deeply we penetrate into matter, by means of increasingly powerful methods, the more we are confounded by the interdependence of its parts. . . . It is impossible to cut into this network, to isolate a portion without it becoming frayed and unravelled at all its edges.

Interestingly enough, this concept of modern physics that the world is in some ways similar to a giant atom is, as far as it goes (and it really is only scratching the surface), the Buddhist doctrine of the "Dharmadhatu," which means Universal Realm or Field of Reality. The major principle of the Dharmadhatu is called *shih shih wu ai*. *Shih* means "thing, event, entity, phenomenon, object, process"; *su* means "no"; and *ai* means "obstruction, block, boundary, separation." *Shih shih wu ai* thus translates as, "Between every thing and event in the universe there is no boundary." Because there are no real dividing boundaries between things, every entity in the world is said to interpenetrate every other entity in the world. As Garma Chang explains:

> In the infinite Dharmadhatu, each and every thing simultaneously includes all (other things) in perfect completion, without the slightest deficiency or omission, at all times. To see one object is, therefore, to see all objects, and vice versa. This is to say a tiny individual particle within the minute cosmos of an atom actually contains the infinite objects and principles in the infinite universes of the future and of the remote past in the perfect completeness without omission.

In Mahayana Buddhism the universe is therefore likened to a vast net of jewels, wherein the reflection from one jewel is contained in all jewels, and the reflections of all are contained in each. As the Buddhists put it, "All in one and one in all." This sounds very mystical and far-out, until you hear a modern physicist explain the present-day view of elementary particles: "This states, in ordinary language, that each particle consists of all the other particles, each of which is in the same way and at the same time all other particles together."

Similarities such as these have prompted many scientists to agree with physicist Fritjof Capra: "The two basic theories of modern physics thus exhibit all the main features of the Eastern world view. Quantum theory has abolished the notion of fundamentally separated objects, has introduced the concept of the participator to replace that of the observer, and has come to see the universe as an interconnected web of relations whose parts are only defined through their connections to the whole." In essence, the great similarity is that both modern science and Eastern philosophy view reality not as boundaries and separate things but as a nondual network of inseparable patterns, a giant atom, a seamless coat of no-boundary.

The reason the East knew this long before Western science stumbled on it is that the East never took boundaries seriously. Boundaries didn't so go to their heads that their heads and nature parted ways. For the East, there was only one Way, the Tao, the Dharma, and it signalled a wholeness under the dividing boundaries of manmade maps. The East, in seeing that reality was nondual, not-two, saw that all boundaries were illusory. Thus, they never really fell into the fallacy of confusing the map with the territory, boundaries with reality, symbols with actuality, names with what is named. Open any good Buddhist sutra, most of which were written centuries ago, and you might read something like this: "By appearance is meant that which reveals itself to the senses and to the discriminating-mind and is perceived as form, sound, odor, taste, and touch. Out of these appearances ideas are formed, such as clay, water, jar, etc., by which one says: this is such and such a thing and is no other,—this is name. When appearances are contrasted and names compared, as when we say: this is an elephant, this is a horse, a cart, a pedestrian, a man, a woman, or, this is mind and what belongs to it,—the things thus named are said to be discriminated. As these discriminations [i.e., boundaries] come to be seen as empty of self-substance, this is right knowledge. By it the wise cease to regard appearances and names as reality. When appearances and names are put away and all discrimination ceases, that which remains is the true and essential nature of things and, as nothing can be predicated as to the nature of essence, it is called the 'Suchness' of Reality. This universal, undifferentiated, inscrutable, 'Suchness' is the only Reality" *(Lankavatara Sutra).*

From another angle, this is the profound Buddhist doctrine of the Void, which maintains that reality is void of thoughts and void of things. It is void of things because, as our physicists discovered, things are simply abstract boundaries of experience. And it is void of thought because thought, our symbolic map-making, is precisely the process which superimposes boundaries on reality. To see a "thing" is to think; to think is to picture "things" to yourself—"thinking" and "thinging" are thus two different names for the net of boundaries we toss over reality.

Hence, when Buddhists say reality is void, they mean it is void of boundaries. They do not mean that all entities simply up and vanish, leaving behind a pure vacuum of nothingness, an undifferentiated monistic mush. Speaking of the Void, D. T. Suzuki says that it "does not deny the world of multiplicities; mountains are there, the cherries are in full bloom, the moon shines most brightly in the autumnal night; but at the same time they are more than particularities, they appeal to us with a deeper meaning, they are understood in relation to what they are not."

The point is that when the world is seen to be void of boundaries, then all things and events—just like all the opposites—are seen to be mutually dependent and interpenetrating. Just as pleasure is related to pain, good to evil, and life to death, so all things are "related to what they are not."

This is difficult for most of us to grasp, for we are still very much under the spell of Adam's original sin, and so we cling to boundaries as if to life itself. But the essence of the insight that reality is no-boundary is very simple. Its simplicity is what makes it so difficult to see. Take, for example, your own visual field. As your eye scans the territory of nature, does it ever see a *single* thing, a solitary thing, a separate thing? Has it ever seen *a* tree? *a* wave? *a* bird? Or does it instead see a kaleidoscopic flux of all sorts of interwoven patterns and textures, of tree plus sky plus grass plus ground, and waves plus sand plus rocks plus sky and clouds. . . .

Even as you now read the lines of print in this book, if you carefully notice your entire visual field, you will see that your eye isn't taking in just one word at a time. Your eye sees, although it can't actually read, all the words on this page, plus some of the surrounding background, perhaps your hands and lower arms, your lap, a table, parts of the room, and so on.

In your immediate and concrete awareness, therefore, there are no separate things, no boundaries. You never actually *see* a single entity, but always a richly textured field. That is the nature of your immediate reality, and it is completely void of boundaries.

But you can mentally superimpose pretend boundaries upon your immediate field of awareness. You can bound off a section of the field by focusing attention on just a few prominent areas, such as "a" tree, "a" wave, "a" bird, and then *pretend* to be aware of just that particular object by deliberately excluding the rest of the field of awareness. You can, that is, *concentrate,* which means to introduce a boundary to awareness. You can focus on just these words and pretend not to notice all the other sights in your conscious field.

This is an extremely useful, and certainly necessary, trick, but it is apt to backfire. The fact that you can concentrate and thus attend to "one separate thing" at a time is liable to make it appear that reality itself is composed of a bunch of these "separate things," while in actuality all these separate things are merely a by-product of your own superimposing boundaries on the field of your awareness. If the only tool you have is a hammer, then everything starts to look like a nail. But the fact is that you never really see boundaries, you only manufacture them. You do not perceive separate things, you invent them. The problem begins as soon as these inventions are mistaken for reality itself, for then the actual world appears as if it were a fragmented and disjointed affair, and a primal mood of alienation invades awareness itself.

So when the Eastern sage says that all things are void, or all things are not-two, or all things are interpenetrating, she does not mean to deny differences, to overlook individuality, to see the world as homogeneous gunk. The world contains all types of features and surfaces and lines, but they are all interwoven into a seamless field. Look at it this way: your hand is surely different from your head, and your head is different from your feet, and your feet are different from your ears. But we have no difficulty at all recognizing that they are all members of one body, and likewise, your one body expresses itself in all its various parts. All-in-one and one-in-all. Similarly, in the territory of no-boundary, all things and events are equally members of one body, the Dharmakaya, the mystical body of Christ, the universal field of Brahman, the organic pattern of the Tao. Any physicist will tell you that all objects in the cosmos are simply various forms of a single Energy—and whether we call that Energy "Brahman," "Tao," "God," or just plain "Energy" seems to me quite beside the point.

What we have seen in the last two chapters—at least according to some of the recent developments in modern science and the ancient wisdom of the East—is that reality is no-boundary. Any conceivable sort of boundary is a mere abstraction from the seamless coat of the universe, and hence all boundaries are pure illusions in the sense that they create separation (and ultimately conflict) where there is none. The boundaries between opposites, as well as the boundaries between things and events, remain at last deceptions in depth.

For the East, the reality of no-boundary has never been just a theoretical or philosophical concern, however. It was never something to be worked out on a blackboard or in a lab, important as these pursuits are. Rather, no-boundary was a matter of everyday, concrete living. For people are always trying to *bound* their lives, their experiences, their realities. And, alas, every boundary line is a potential battle line. Thus, the sole aim of the Eastern (and esoteric Western) ways of liberation is to deliver people from the conflicts and complexities of their battles by delivering them from their boundaries. They do not try to solve the battle in its own terms, for that is as impossible as washing off blood with blood. Instead, they simply demonstrate the illusory nature of the boundaries which create the battles. Thus the battle is not solved, but dissolved.

To disclose reality as no-boundary is thus to disclose all conflicts as illusory. And this final understanding is called nirvana, moksha, release, liberation, enlightenment, satori—freed from the pairs, freed from the enchanting vision of separateness, freed from the chains of one's illusory boundaries. And with this understanding, we are now ready to examine this no-boundary awareness, commonly called "unity consciousness."

4

No-Boundary Awareness

UNITY CONSCIOUSNESS is the simple awareness of the real territory of no-boundary. We need no gimmicks to explain it, no
mumbo-jumbo, no mystical jargon, no miasma of occultism. If reality is
actually a condition of no-boundary—and to deny that we will have to
turn our backs on Relativity Theory, ecological sciences, the philosophy
of organism, and the wisdom of the East—if reality is a condition of no-
boundary, then unity consciousness is the natural state of awareness
which acknowledges this reality. Unity consciousness, in short, is no-
boundary awareness.

As simple as that sounds, it is nevertheless extremely difficult to adequately discuss no-boundary awareness or nondual consciousness. This
is because our language—the medium in which all verbal discussion
must float—is a language of boundaries. As we have seen, words and
symbols and thoughts themselves are actually nothing but boundaries,
for whenever you think or use a word or name, you are already creating
boundaries. Even to say "reality is no-boundary awareness" is still to
create a distinction between boundaries and no-boundary! So we have
to keep in mind the great difficulty involved with dualistic language.
That "reality is no-boundary" is true enough, provided we remember
that no-boundary awareness is a direct, immediate, and nonverbal
awareness, and not a mere philosophical theory. It is for these reasons
that the mystic-sages stress that reality lies beyond names and forms,
words and thoughts, divisions and boundaries. Beyond all boundaries
lies the real world of Suchness, the Void, the Dharmakaya, Tao, Brah-

man, the Godhead. And in the world of suchness, there is neither good nor bad, saint nor sinner, birth nor death, for in the world of suchness there are no boundaries.

And especially there is no boundary between subject and object, self and not-self, seer and seen. I emphasize that point, and will dwell on it throughout this chapter, because of all the boundaries we construct, the one between self and not-self is the most fundamental. It is the boundary we are most reluctant to surrender. It was, after all, the first boundary we ever drew. It is our most cherished boundary. We have invested years to fortify it and defend it, make it secure and safe. It is the very boundary that establishes our sense of being a separate self. And as we grow old, full of years and memories, and begin to slip into the nothingness of death, this is the last boundary we relinquish. The boundary between self and not-self is the first one we draw and the last one we erase. Of all the boundaries we construct, this one is the primary boundary.

So fundamental is the primary boundary between self and not-self that all our other boundaries depend on it. We can hardly distinguish boundaries between things until we have distinguished ourselves *from* things. Every boundary *you* create depends upon *your* separate existence, that is, your primary boundary of self vs. not-self.

To be sure, any and all boundaries are obstacles to unity consciousness, but, since all of our other boundaries depend upon this primary boundary, to see through it is to see through all. In a sense this is most fortunate, for if we had to tackle all of our boundaries separately, one by one, it would take a lifetime, perhaps several, to dissolve them all and gain "liberation from the pairs." But by aiming at the primary boundary, our work is enormously simplified. It is as if our various boundaries constituted an inverted pyramid of blocks, all of which are resting on the one block at the tip. Pull out that one block and the whole edifice collapses.

We can look at this primary boundary from many angles, and under many names. It is that irreducible separation between what I call myself and what I call not-self, me in here and objects out there. It is the split between the knowing subject and the known object. It is that space between my organism and the environment. It is the gap between the "I" which is now reading and the page which is being read. All in all, it is the gap between the experiencer and the world which is experienced. It thus appears that on the "inside" of the primary boundary there exists my "self," the subject, the thinker and feeler and seer; and on the other side there exists the not-self, the world of objects out there, the environment, foreign and separate from me.

In unity consciousness, in no-boundary awareness, the sense of self expands to totally include everything once thought to be not-self. One's sense of identity shifts to the entire universe, to all worlds, high or low, manifest or unmanifest, sacred or profane. And obviously this cannot occur as long as the primary boundary, which *separates* the self from the universe, is mistaken as real. But once the primary boundary is understood to be illusory, one's sense of self envelops the All—there is then no longer anything outside of oneself, and so nowhere to draw any sort of boundary. Thus, if we can at all begin to see through the primary boundary, the sense of unity consciousness will not be far from us.

From the foregoing it's too easy to jump to the erroneous conclusion that all we have to do to usher in unity consciousness is destroy the primary boundary. In a crude sense that is true, but the situation is actually much, much simpler than that. We really don't have to go to the trouble of trying to destroy the primary boundary, and for an extremely simple reason: the primary boundary doesn't exist.

Like all boundaries, it is only an illusion. It only *seems* to exist. We pretend it exists, we assume it exists, we behave in every way as if it exists. But it does not. And if we now go in search of the primary boundary, we will not find a trace of it, for ghosts leave no shadows. Right now, and I mean right while you're reading this, there is no real primary boundary, and so right now, there is no real barrier to unity consciousness.

Thus, we will not search out the primary boundary and then try to destroy it. That, in fact, would be a grave error, or at least a colossal waste of time, for we cannot destroy what doesn't exist in the first place. Trying to destroy the primary boundary is like standing in the midst of a mirage and batting one's arms furiously in an attempt to dispel it— despite the intense excitement such activity may generate, it remains a totally futile affair. You cannot eradicate an illusion. You can only understand and see through the illusion itself. From this point of view, even trying to destroy the primary boundary through such elaborate activities as yoga, mental concentration, prayer, ritual, chanting, fasting—all of that merely assumes the primary boundary to be real and thereby enforces and perpetuates the very illusion it seeks to destroy. As Fenelon, Archbishop of Cambrai, put it, "There is no more dangerous illusion than the fancies by which people try to avoid illusion."

Instead of assuming the primary boundary to be real and then taking steps to try to eliminate it, we will first go in search of the primary boundary itself. And if it indeed is an illusion, we will never find a trace of it. We might then *spontaneously* understand that what we thought obstructed our unity consciousness never existed in the first place. And, as we shall see, that insight itself is already a glimpse of no-boundary awareness.

Now what exactly does it mean to look for the primary boundary? To look for the primary boundary is to look very carefully for the sensation of being a separate self, a separate experiencer and feeler which is set apart from experiences and feelings. I am suggesting that if we carefully look for this "self," we won't find it. And since this feeling of being an isolated self seems to be the major obstacle to unity consciousness, to look for it and not find it is, at the same time, to glimpse unity consciousness itself. Listen to the great Buddhist sage Padmasambhava: "If the seeker himself, when sought, cannot be found, thereupon is attained the goal of seeking and also the end of the search itself."

At the outset of such an experiment, we must be very clear about just what this "absence of self" or "absence of primary boundary" means. It does not mean a loss of all sensibilities; it is not a state of trance, chaos, turmoil, or uncontrolled behavior. It is not that my mind and body explode into vapor and merge into One Large Lump of some sort of something somewhere. It has nothing to do with schizophrenic regression, which does not transcend the self/not-self boundary at all, but instead muddles and confuses it.

Rather, when we speak of "loss of self" we mean this: The sensation of being a separate self is a sensation that has been misunderstood and misinterpreted, and it is the dispelling of this misinterpretation that concerns us. We all have that sensation, that core feeling, of being an isolated self split from our stream of experience and split from the world around us. We all have the feeling of "self" on the one hand and the feeling of the external world on the other. But if we carefully look at the sensation of "self-in-here" and the sensation of "world-out-there," we will find that these two sensations are actually *one and the same feeling*. In other words, what I now feel to be the objective world out there *is* the same thing I feel to be the subjective self in here. The split between the experiencer and the world of experiences does not exist, and therefore cannot be found. . . .

Initially this sounds very strange, because we are so used to believing in boundaries. It seems so obvious that I am the hearer who hears sounds, that I am the feeler who feels feelings, that I am the seer who sees sights. But, on the other hand, isn't it odd that I should describe myself as the *seer* who *sees* the things *seen?* Or the *hearer* who *hears* the sounds *heard?* Is perception really that complicated? Does it really involve three separate entities—a seer, seeing, and the seen?

Surely there aren't three separate entities here. Is there ever such a thing as a seer without seeing or without something seen? Is there ever seeing without a seer or without something seen? The fact is, the seer, seeing, and the seen are all aspects of one process—never at any time is one of them found without the others.

Our problem is that we have three words—the "seer," "sees," and the "seen"—for one single activity, the experience of seeing. We might as well describe a single water stream as "the streamer streams the streamed." It is utterly redundant, and introduces three factors where there is in fact but one. Yet, hypnotized as we are by Adam's word magic, we assume there must be a separate entity, the seer, and that through some sort of process called "seeing," the "seer" gains knowledge of yet another thing called the "seen." We then naturally assume that we are *just* the seer which is totally divorced from the seen. Our world, which is only given once, is thereby split right down the middle, with the "seer in here" confronting, across a gaping abyss, the things "seen out there."

Let us instead go back to the very beginning of the process of experience itself, and see if the experiencer is really all that different from the experienced. Begin with the sense of hearing. Close your eyes and attend to the actual process of hearing. Notice all the odd sounds floating around—birds singing, cars rumbling, crickets chirping, kids laughing, TV blaring. But with all those sounds, notice that there is one thing which you cannot hear, no matter how carefully you attend to every sound. You cannot hear the hearer. That is, in addition to those sounds, you cannot hear a hearer of those sounds.

You cannot hear a hearer *because there isn't one.* What you have been taught to call a "hearer" is actually just the experience of hearing itself, and you don't hear hearing. In reality, there is just a stream of sounds, and that stream is not split into a subject and an object. There is no boundary here.

If you let the sensation of being a "hearer" inside the skull dissolve into hearing itself, you might find your "self" merging with the entire world of "outside sounds." As one Zen Master exclaimed upon his enlightenment, "When I heard the temple bell ring, suddenly there was no bell and no I, just the ringing." It was through such an experiment that

Avalokiteshvara is said to have gained his enlightenment, for in giving awareness to the process of hearing, he realized that there was no separate self, no hearer, apart from the stream of hearing itself. When you try to hear the *subjective* hearer, all you find are *objective* sounds. And that means that you do not hear sounds, you *are* those sounds. The hearer *is* every sound which is heard. It is not a separate entity which stands back and hears hearing.

The same is true of the process of seeing. As I look carefully at the visual field, it seems almost to hang in space, suspended in nothingness. Yet it consists of an infinitely rich pattern of interlaced lights, colors, and shades, forming themselves into a mountain here, a cloud there, a stream below. But of all the sights I can see, there is still that one thing which I cannot see, no matter how the eyes strain. I cannot see the seer of this visual field.

The more I try to see the seer, the more its absence begins to puzzle me. For years it seemed perfectly natural to assume that I was the seer which saw sights. But the moment I go in search of the seer, I find no trace of it. In fact, if I persist in trying to see the seer, *all* I find are things which are *seen*. This simply means that I, the "seer," do not see sights—rather I, the "seer," am identical to all those sights now present. The so-called seer is nothing other than everything which is seen. If I look at a tree, there is not one experience called "tree" and another experience called "seeing the tree." There is just the single experience of seeing-the-tree. I do not see this seeing any more than I smell smelling or taste tasting.

It seems that whenever we look for a self apart from experience, it vanishes *into* experience. When we look for the experiencer, we find only another experience—the subject and object always turn out to be one. Because this is a rather unnerving experience, you might now be feeling somewhat confused, as you sit thinking all of this over. But push onward just a bit. As you are now thinking about this, can you also find a thinker who is thinking about this?

That is, is there a thinker who thinks the thought, "I am confused," or is there just the thought, "I am confused"? Surely there is just the present thought, because if there were also a thinker of the thought, would you then think about the thinker who is thinking the thought? It seems obvious that what we mistakenly believe to be a thinker is really nothing other than the stream of present thoughts.

Thus, when the present thought was "I am confused," you were not *at the same time* aware of a thinker who was thinking, "I am confused."

There was *just* the present thought alone—"I am confused." When you *then* looked for the thinker of that thought, all you found was *another* present thought, namely "I am thinking I am confused." Never did you find a thinker apart from the present thought, which is only to say that the two are identical.

This is precisely why the sages advise us not to try to destroy the "self," but simply to look for it, because whenever we look for it all we find is its prior absence. But even if we have begun to understand that there is no separate hearer, no taster, no seer, and no thinker, we are still likely to find within ourselves a type of irreducible, core feeling of being a separate and isolated self. There is still that sensation of being separate from the world out there. There is still that gut feeling that I somehow know as my inner "self." Even if I can't see, taste, or hear my self, I definitely *feel* my self.

Well, can you find, *in addition* to the feeling you are now calling your "self," a *feeler* who is doing the feeling? If it seems that you can, can you then feel the feeler who is doing the feeling? Again, that core sensation of being a feeler who has feelings is itself *just another feeling*. The "feeler" is nothing but a present feeling, just as the thinker is just a present thought and the taster is just present tastes. In this case, too, there is no separate feeler different from present feelings—and there never was.

Thus the inescapable conclusion starts to dawn on us: there is no separate self set apart from the world. You have always assumed you were a separate experiencer, but the moment you actually go in search of it, it vanishes *into* experience. As Alan Watts puts it, "There is simply experience. There is not something or someone experiencing experience! You do not feel feeling, think thoughts, or sense sensations any more than you hear hearing, see sight, or smell smelling. 'I feel fine' means that a fine feeling is present. It does not mean that there is one thing called an 'I' and another separate thing called a feeling, so that when you bring them together this 'I' *feels* the fine feelings. There are no feelings but present feelings, and whatever feeling is present is 'I.' No one ever found an 'I' apart from some present experience, or some experience apart from an 'I'—which is only to say that the two are the same thing."

Now when you understand that there is no gap between "you" and your experiences, doesn't it start to become obvious that there is no gap between "you" and the world which is experienced? If you are your experiences, you are the world so experienced. You do not have a sensation of a bird, you are the sensation of a bird. You do not have an experience of a table, you are the experience of the table. You do not hear the sound of thunder, you are the sound of thunder. The inner sensation called "you" and the outer sensation called "the world" are one and the same sensation. The inner subject and the outer object are two names for one feeling, and this is not something you *should* feel, it is the only thing you *can* feel.

That means that your state of consciousness right now is, whether you realize it or not, unity consciousness. Right now you *already* are the cosmos, you *already* are the totality of your present experience. Your present state is always unity consciousness because the separate self, which seems to be the major obstacle to unity consciousness, is always an illusion. You needn't try to destroy the separate self because it isn't there in the first place. All you really have to do is look for it, and you won't find it. That very not-finding is itself an acknowledgement of unity consciousness. In other words, whenever you look for your "self" and don't find it, you momentarily fall into your prior and real state of unity consciousness.

As odd as all of this might initially sound, the insight that there is no separate self has been obvious to the mystics and sages of all times, and forms one of the core points of the perennial philosophy. Although there are numerous quotations that could illustrate this insight, the celebrated summary of the Buddha's teachings really says it all:

> Suffering alone exists, none who suffer;
> The deed there is, but no doer thereof;
> Nirvana is, but no one seeking it;
> The Path there is, but none who travel it.

And it is just that understanding which is universally said to constitute liberation from all suffering. Stated positively: when it is realized that one's self is the All, there is then nothing outside of oneself which *could* inflict suffering. There is nothing outside of the universe against which it might crash. Stated negatively: this understanding is a liberation from all suffering because it is a liberation from the notion that there is a self which *can* suffer in the first place. As Wei Wu Wei put it:

> Why are you unhappy?
> Because 99.9 percent
> Of everything you think, and
> Of everything you do,
> Is for yourself—
> And there isn't one.

Only parts suffer, not the Whole. And this realization, when stated "negatively" by the mystics, says, "You are released from suffering when you realize the part is an illusion—there is no separate self to suffer." When stated "positively," it says, "You are always the Whole, which knows only freedom, release, and radiance. To realize the Whole is to escape the fate of a part, which is only suffering, pain, and death." Hinayana Buddhism stresses the former, Hinduism and Christianity the latter, and Mahayana Buddhism seems to strike a happy balance. Yet they are all witness to the same insight.

When we realize there is no part, we fall into the Whole. When we realize that there is always no self (and this is happening right now) we realize that our true identity is always the Supreme Identity. In the ever-present light of no-boundary awareness, what we once imagined to be the isolated self in here turns out to be all of a piece with the cosmos out there. And this, if anything, is your real self. Wherever you look, you behold your original face on all sides.

> I came back into the hall [as one Zen Master explained his first glimpse of no-boundary] and was about to go to my seat when the whole outlook changed. As I looked around and up and down, the whole universe with its multitudinous sense-objects now appeared quite different; what was loathsome before, together with ignorance and passions, was now seen to be nothing else but the outflow of my own inmost nature which in itself remained bright, true, and transparent.

Tat tvam asi, the Hindus say. "You are That. Your real Self is identical to the ultimate Energy of which all things in the universe are a manifestation."

This real self has been given dozens of different names by the various mystical and metaphysical traditions throughout human history. It had been known as the al-Insan al-Kamil, Adam Kadmon, Ruach Adonai, Nous, Pneuma, Purusha, Tathagatagarbha, Universal Person, the Host, the Brahman-Atman, I AMness. And from a slightly different angle, it is actually synonymous with the Dharmadhatu, the Void, Suchness, and the Godhead. All of these words are simply symbols of the real world of no-boundary.

Now the real self is frequently referred to by some sort of appellation suggesting that it is the "innermost" core of humans, that it is preeminently subjective, inner, personal, nonobjective, inside, and within. We are told unanimously by the mystics that "the Kingdom of Heaven is within," that we are to search the depths of our souls until we uncover, hidden in our innermost being, the Real Self of all existence. As Swami Prabhavananda used to say, "Who, what, do you think you are? Absolutely, basically, fundamentally deep within?"

One will often find the real self referred to as something like the "inner Witness," the "Absolute Seer and Knower," one's "Innermost Nature," "Absolute Subjectivity," and so on. Thus Shankara, master of Vedanta Hinduism, would say, "There is a self-existent Reality, which is the basis of our consciousness of ego. That Reality is the Witness of the three states of consciousness [waking, dreaming, sleeping], and is distinct from the five bodily coverings. That Reality is the Knower in all states of consciousness. It is aware of the presence or absence of the mind. This is Atman, the Supreme Being, the ancient." Or take this excellent quote from Zen Master Shibayama:

> It (Reality) is "Absolute Subjectivity," which transcends both subjectivity and objectivity and freely creates and uses them. It is "Fundamental Subjectivity," which can never be objectified or conceptualized and is complete in itself, with the full significance of existence in itself. To call it by these names is already a mistake, a step toward objectification and conceptualization. Master Eisai therefore remarked, "It is ever unnamable."
>
> The Absolute Subjectivity that can never be objectified or conceptualized is free from the limitations of space and time; it is not subject to life and death; it goes beyond subject and object, and although it lives in an individual it is not restricted to the individual.

But in saying that the real self is the True Seer, or Inner Witness, or Absolute Subjectivity within each of us might seem contradictory in light of what we have said thus far about unity consciousness. For, on the one hand, we have seen that the real self is an ever-present no-boundary awareness wherein the subject and the object, the seer and the seen, the experiencer and the experienced form a single continuum. Yet, on the other hand, we have just described the real self as the inner Witness, the ultimate Knower. We said it is the Seer and not the seen, it is inside and not outside. What are we to make of this seeming contradiction?

First we must recognize the difficulties the mystic faces in trying to describe the ineffable experience of unity consciousness. Foremost among these is the fact that the real self is a no-boundary awareness, whereas all our words and thoughts are nothing but boundaries. This, however, is not a flaw confined to any particular language, but is inherent in all languages by virtue of their very structure. A language possesses utility only insofar as it can construct conventional boundaries. A language of no boundaries is no language at all, and thus the mystic who tries to speak logically and formally of unity consciousness is doomed to sound very paradoxical or contradictory. The problem is that the structure of any language cannot grasp the nature of unity consciousness, any more than a fork could grasp the ocean.

So the mystics must be content with pointing and showing a Way whereby we may all experience unity consciousness for ourselves. In this sense, the mystic path is a purely experimental one. The mystics ask you to believe nothing on blind faith, to accept no authority but that of your own understanding and experience. They ask you only to try a few experiments in awareness, to look closely at your present state of existence, and to try to see your self and your world as clearly as you possibly can. Don't think, just look! as Wittgenstein exclaimed.

But just *where* to look? This is precisely the point at which the mystics universally answers, "Look inside. Deep inside. For the real self lies within." Now the mystics are not *describing* the real self as *being inside* you—they are *pointing* inside you. They are indeed saying to look within, not because the final answer actually resides within you and not without, but because as you carefully and consistently look inside, you sooner or later find outside. You realize, in other words, that the inside and the outside, the subject and the object, the seer and the seen are one, and thus you spontaneously fall into your natural state. So the mystic begins by talking of real self in a way that seems contradictory to everything we earlier said. However, if we follow the mystic through to the end, the conclusion—as we will see—is identical.

Start by considering what something like "Absolute Subjectivity" or "Inner Witness" might mean, at least the way the mystic uses it. Absolute Subjectivity would be that which can never, at any time, under any circumstances, be a particular object that can be seen, or heard, or known, or perceived. As the absolute Seer, it could never be seen. As the absolute Knower, it could never be known. Lao Tzu speaks of it thus:

> Because the eye gazes but can catch no glimpse of it,
> It is called elusive.
> Because the ear listens but cannot hear it,
> It is called the rarefied.
> Because the hand feels for it but cannot find it,
> It is called the infinitesimal.

In order to contact this real self or Absolute Subjectivity, most mystics therefore proceed with something like the following from Sri Ramana Maharshi: "The gross body which is composed of the seven humors, *I am not;* the five sense organs which apprehend their respective objects, *I am not;* even the mind which thinks, *I am not."*

But what, then, could this real self be? As Ramana pointed out, it can't be my body, because I can feel and know it, and what can be known is not the absolute Knower. It can't be my wishes, hopes fears, and emotions, for I can to some degree see and feel them, and what can be seen is not the absolute Seer. It can't be my mind, my personality, my thoughts, for those can all be witnessed, and what can be witnessed is not the absolute Witness.

By persistently looking within for the real self in this fashion, I am, in fact, starting to realize that it cannot be found within at all. I used to think of myself as the "little subject" in here who watched all those objects out there. But the mystic shows me clearly that this "little sub-ject" can in fact be seen as an *object!* It's not a real subject, my real self, at all.

But just here, according to the mystic, is our major problem in life and living. For most of us imagine that we can feel ourselves, or know ourselves, or perceive ourselves, or at least be aware of ourselves in some sense. We have that feeling even now. But, replies that mystic, the fact that I can see, or know, or feel my "self" at this moment shows me conclusively that this "self" cannot be my real self at all. It's a false self, a pseudo-self, an illusion and a hoax. We have inadvertently identified with a complex of *objects,* all of which we know or can know. There-fore, this complex of knowable objects cannot be the true Knower or real Self. We have identified ourselves with our body, mind, and person-ality, imagining these objects to constitute our real "self," and we then spend our entire lives trying to defend, protect, and prolong what is just an illusion.

We are the victims of an epidemic case of mistaken identity, with our Supreme Identity quietly but surely awaiting discovery. And the mystics want nothing more than to have us awaken to who, or what, we really and eternally are *beneath* or *under* or *prior to* our pseudo-self. Thus they ask us to cease identifying with this false self, to realize that whatever I can know, think, or feel about myself cannot constitute my real Self.

My mind, my body, my thoughts, my desires—these are no more my real Self than the trees, the stars, the clouds, and the mountains, for I can witness *all* of them as objects, with equal felicity. Proceeding in this fashion, I become transparent to my Self, and realize that in some sense what I am goes much, much beyond this isolated, skin-bounded organism. The more I go into I, the more I fall out of I.

As this investigation is pushed, a curious flip in consciousness occurs, which the *Lankavatara Sutra* calls "a turning about in the deepest seat of consciousness." The more I look for the absolute Seer, the more I realize that I can't find it as an object. And the simple reason I can't find it as a particular object is because it's *every* object! I can't feel it because it *is* everything felt. I can't experience it because it is everything experienced. It is true that anything I can see is *not* the Seer—because everything I see is the Seer. As I go within to find my real self, I find only the world.

But a strange thing has now happened, for I realize that the real self within is actually the real world without, and vice versa. The subject and object, the inside and outside, are and always have been nondual. There is no primary boundary. The world is my body, and what I am looking out of is what I am looking at.

Because the real self resides neither within nor without, because the subject and object are actually not-two, the mystics can speak of reality in many different but only apparently contradictory ways. They can say that in all reality there are no objects whatsoever. Or, they might state that reality contains no subjects at all. Or they can deny the existence of both subject and object. Or they may speak of an Absolute Subjectivity which transcends yet includes both the relative subject and the relative object. All of these are simply various ways of saying that the inside world and the outside world are just two different names for the single, ever-present state of no-boundary awareness.

Perhaps it is now obvious that, despite the complex theoretical formulations which often surround the perennial philosophy, the essence of the mystical message is plain, simple, and straightforward. To look back: In chapter two we saw that reality is a union of opposites, or "nondual." Since it is symbolic maps and boundaries which appear to separate the opposites into conflicting enemies, to say reality is nondual is to say reality is no-boundary.

In chapter three, we saw that the real world is not a collection of separate and independent things divorced from one another in space and time. Every thing and event in the cosmos is mutually interdependent and interrelated with every other thing and event in the cosmos. And once again, because it is our symbolic maps and boundaries which present us with the illusion of independent entities, to say the real world contains no separate things is to say that the real world is no-boundary.

In this chapter, we saw that the discovery of the real world of no-boundary *is* unity consciousness. It is not that in unity consciousness you are looking at the real territory of no-boundary; rather, unity consciousness *is* the real territory of no-boundary. Reality, by all accounts, is no-boundary awareness—that just that is one's Real Self. "Thus," to quote the founder of quantum mechanics, Erwin Schroedinger, "you can throw yourself flat on the ground, stretched out upon Mother Earth, with the certain conviction that you are one with her and she with you. You are as firmly established, as invulnerable as she, indeed a thousand times firmer and more invulnerable. As surely as she will engulf you tomorrow, so surely will she bring you forth anew to new striving and suffering. And not merely 'some day': now, today, every day she is bringing you forth, not *once* but thousands of times, just as every day she engulfs you a thousand times over. For eternally and always there is only *now*, one and the same now; the present is the only thing that has no end."

5

The No-Boundary Moment

"Need there is, methinks, to understand the sense in which the scripture speaketh of time and eternity." With those words, St. Dionysius put his finger on the whole crux of mystical insight, for the enlightened sages of all times and places agree that unity consciousness is not temporal, not of time, but eternal, timeless. It knows no beginning, no birth, and no ending, no death. Thus, until we thoroughly grasp the nature of eternity, the sense of the Real will elude us.

"Who," asks St. Augustine, "will hold the heart of man that it may stand still and see how eternity, ever still-standing, neither past nor to come, uttereth the times past and to come?" Who indeed? For grasping that which is eternal—if in fact such even exists—seems so weighty, momentous, and well nigh impossible a task that we are likely to shrink before it. Modern individuals seem so generally bereft of even the least mystical insight that they shrug off the notion of eternity altogether, or explain it away with a positivistic fury, or demand to know what it has to do with "practical reality."

Yet the mystic claims that eternity is not a philosophical opinion, nor a religious dogma, nor an unattainable ideal. Eternity rather is so simple, so obvious, so present, and so straightforward that we have only to open our eyes in a radically empirical fashion and *look*. As Zen Master Huang Po used to repeatedly stress, "It's right in front of you!"

Part of the reason that "contacting the eternal" seems so awesome is that we generally misunderstand the true sense of the word "eternity" itself. We commonly imagine eternity to be a very, very long time, an unending stretch of years, a million times a million forever. But the mystic does not understand eternity in that fashion at all. For eternity is not an awareness of *everlasting time,* but an awareness which is itself *totally without time.* The eternal moment is a timeless moment, a moment which knows neither past nor future, before nor after, yesterday nor tomorrow, birth nor death. To live in unity consciousness is to live in and as the timeless moment, for nothing obscures the divine light more thoroughly than the taint of time. As Meister Eckhart put it, "Time is what keeps the light from reaching us. There is no greater obstacle to God [unity consciousness] than time. And not only time but temporalities, not only temporal things but temporal affectations; not only temporal affectations but the very taint and smell of time."

And yet, we must ask, what is a timeless moment? What instant is without date or duration? What moment is not just quick or short-lived in time, but absolutely without time?

Odd as these questions initially seem, most of us would have to admit that we have known moments, peak moments, which seemed indeed to lie so far beyond time that the past and the future melted away into obscurity. Lost in a sunset; transfixed by the play of moonlight on a crystal dark pond which possesses no bottom; floated out of self and time in the enraptured embrace of a loved one; caught and held still-bound by the crack of thunder echoing through mists of rain. Who has not touched the timeless?

What do all of these experiences have in common? It seems, and the mystic agrees, that time appears suspended in all of these experiences because we are totally absorbed in the *present moment.* Clearly, in this present moment, if we would but examine it, there is no time. The present moment is a timeless moment, and a timeless moment is an eternal one—a moment which knows neither past nor future, before nor after, yesterday nor tomorrow. To enter deeply into this present moment is thus to plunge into eternity, to step through the looking glass and into the world of the Unborn and the Undying.

For there is *no beginning* to *this* present moment, and that which has no beginning is the Unborn. That is, search as you will, you cannot find, see, or feel a *beginning* to your experience of this present moment. When did this present begin? Did it ever begin? Or could it possibly be that this present floats so above time that it never entered the temporal stream at *any* beginning? In the same vein, there is *no ending* to *this* present moment, and that which has no ending is the Undying. Again, search as you will, you cannot find, see, or feel an *ending* to your experience of this present moment. You never experience an ending to the present (even if you die—since you would not be there to feel anything end). This is why we heard Schroedinger say that "the present is the only thing that has no end." Granted that the outer forms of the present moment cascade by in bewildering succession, still the present itself remains indestructible, untouched by what we have been taught to interpret as "time." In this present moment there is neither past nor future—there is no time. And that which is timeless is eternal. Says Zen Master Seppo, "If you want to know what eternity means, it is no further than this very moment. If you fail to catch it in this present moment, you will not get it, however many times you are reborn in hundreds of thousands of years."

So the notion of everlasting time is a monstrosity—impossible to actually conceive, grasp, or experience in any way whatsoever. But the eternal now, *this* timeless moment, is as simple and as accessible as your own present experience—for the two are one and the same. Thus, said Wittgenstein, "eternal life belongs to those who live in the present."

Because eternity is the nature of *this* present and timeless moment, the mystic tells us that the great liberation, the entrance to the Kingdom of Heaven, the very portal leading "beyond the pairs of past and future," exists nowhere and nowhen else but now. In the words of the Christian sage de Caussade, "O all ye who thirst! Know that you have not far to seek for the fountain of living waters; it springs close to you in the present moment. . . . The present moment is the manifestation of the Name of God and the coming of the Kingdom." Hence, says the Muslim mystic Rumi, "the Sufi is a child of the Moment." Such quotes could go on forever, taken from the words of the great sages of every major religious and philosophical persuasion, but they would all indicate the same thing. Eternity is not, and cannot, be found tomorrow—it is not found in five minutes—it is not found in two seconds. It is always already Now. The present is the only reality. There is no other.

And yet it seems—and for reasons soon apparent I stress the word "seems"—that so few of us live solely and completely in the now. We dwell in yesterdays and dream forever of tomorrows, and thus bind ourselves with the torturous chains of time and the ghosts of things not really present. We dissipate our energies in fantasy mists of memories and expectations, and thus deprive the living present of its fundamental reality and reduce it to a "specious present," a slender present that endures a mere one or two seconds, a pale shadow of the eternal Present. Unable to live in the timeless present and bathe in the delights of eternity, we seek as anemic substitutes the mere promises of time, hoping always that the future will bring what the slender present so piteously lacks.

And this life in time, according to the mystic, is a life in misery. For the mystic claims that all of our problems are problems of time and problems in time. You might never have looked at it this way, but a moment's consideration reveals the utter obviousness of it. All our problems concern time—our worries are always over the past or over the future. We lament many of our past actions and dread their future consequences. Our feelings of guilt are inseparably linked to the past, and bring with them torments of depression, bitterness, and regrets. If this is not clear, then just imagine what it would be like to live without any of the scars of your past. So also, all anxiety is tied to thoughts of the future, and brings with it clouds of dread and catastrophic expectation. The past and the future! These surely are the links in the shackles of our misery. Warns the *Bhagavad Gita:*

> I am come as Time, the waster of peoples,
> Ready for the hour that ripens to their ruin.

And yet, in the strict present there are no fundamental problems—for there is no time. No such animal as a present problem exists—and if there seems to be, a closer examination will inevitably reveal that it is really tied up with some past guilt or some future anxiety. For all guilt is a state of being lost in the past; all anxiety is a state of being lost in the future. It is in this sense that the mystic claims that all our problems are generated by our vivid sensation of, and bondage to, time. As Stephen lamented in *Ulysses,* "History is a nightmare from which I am trying to awaken." And, as Emerson so beautifully pointed out, this awakening occurs only as we become present to the present:

> These roses under my window make no reference to former roses or to better ones; they are for what they are; they exist with God today. There is no time for them. There is simply the rose; it is perfect in every moment of its existence. . . . But man postpones or remembers; he does not live in the present, but with reverted eye laments the past, or heedless of the riches that surround him, stands on tiptoe to foresee the future. He cannot be happy and strong until he too lives with nature in the present, above time.

"To live in the present, above time" and to be a "child of the Moment" thus seems to be the crux of the whole matter of eternity and unity consciousness, for the timeless present is none other than the straight and narrow way which is said to lead "from time to eternity, from death to immortality."

Yet we must be very careful at this point in our understanding. For this "living in the timeless present," this bare attention to the present moment, has nothing to do with the common psychological trick of just forgetting about yesterday and tomorrow. The mystic are not saying that we should live in the present by forgetting about or trying to ignore the past and future. They are saying—and at first this will sound worse—that *there is no past and future*. For the past and future are simply the illusory products of a symbolic boundary superimposed upon the eternal now, a symbolic boundary which appears to split eternity into yesterday vs. tomorrow, before vs. after, time gone vs. time to come. Thus time, as a boundary upon eternity, is not a problem to get rid of, but an illusion which doesn't exist in the first place.

So we must, at this point, be very careful and proceed with utmost caution in order to understand this eternal awareness correctly. Many people, after theoretically grasping that eternity is not everlasting time but the timeless present, try to *contact* this timeless present by concentrating their attention on the now-moment, on whatever they are presently experiencing. They practice "bare attention" to the immediate present in an attempt to contact the timeless now-moment.

But as reasonable as that sounds, it nevertheless is beside the point. For *trying* to contact *this* now-moment still requires *another* now-moment in which this contact might occur. In other words, *trying* to live in the timeless present requires time. Trying to pay attention to the present requires a future in which this attention might be paid. And yet we are not talking about some future in which *this* now-moment is grasped: we are talking of just this now-moment. One cannot, in short, use time to get out of time. By doing so we just reinforce that which we wish to uproot.

This is exasperating only because we constantly assume that we aren't already living in the eternal now, and that therefore we must take steps that will ensure, at some future time, that we will then live as the eternal now. In other words, we assume time is real, and then try to destroy it. Worse, we try to destroy time by time, and that will never work. So, as always, the mystics do not ask us to try to destroy illusions—they ask us only to carefully look for them. For if time actually does not exist, we needn't worry about trying to destroy it. Thus, before we try to get rid of time, let's see if we can find it first. But if we look for time and can't find it, then we will already have glimpsed the timeless.

We have seen that direct experience shows us that there is no separate self standing apart from the world of experience. Likewise, and in just the same way, we will now look to direct experience for any evidence as to whether or not time, the flow from past to future, actually exists.

Let us begin with our senses. Do we ever sense time? That is, do we ever directly sense a past or a future? Start again with hearing. For the moment concentrate your attention on just your auditory field, and notice the flux of sounds kaleidoscoping through your awareness. You might be able to hear people talking, dogs barking, kids playing; perhaps wind blowing, rain splashing, faucet dripping; maybe you can hear the house creaking, or cars honking, or someone laughing. But notice: *all* these sounds are *present* sounds. You cannot hear past sounds, nor can you hear future sounds. *The only thing you ever hear is the present.* You do not and cannot hear a past or future.

Just as all sounds are only present sounds, so all tastes are only present tastes, all smells are present smells, and all sights are present sights. You cannot touch, see, or feel anything resembling a past or a future. In other words, in your direct and immediate awareness, there is no time—no past, no future, only an endlessly changing present, shorter than a minisecond yet never coming to an end. All direct awareness is timeless awareness.

And yet, what is it that gives me the overwhelming impression that I am aware of time, especially of time past, of my whole personal history, of all the things that were? For although I certainly understand that in my direct experience there is no past, only an endless present, I nevertheless am firmly convinced that I know something of the past. And no verbal sleight-of-hand can convince me otherwise, for there is something which speaks clearly and forcefully to me of things which happened minutes ago, days ago, even years ago. What is that? And how can it be denied?

The answer to the first question seems obvious: it is memory. For although I do not directly see the past, nor feel it, nor touch it, I can remember it. Memory alone assures me that there was a past, and, in fact, were it not for memory I would have no idea of time whatsoever. Further, I notice that other people seem to have a memory also, and they all substantially report the same type of past that I recall.

And so, I assume, *memory gives me a knowledge of the actual past,* even if I can't directly experience that past. But right here, claim the mystics, I have made a fatal mistake. The mystics agree that when I think of the past, all I really know is a certain memory—but, they add, *that memory is itself a present experience*. Alan Watts elaborates: "But what about memories? Surely by remembering I can also know what is past? Very well, remember something. Remember the incident of seeing a friend walking down the street. What are you aware of? You are not actually watching the veritable event of your friend walking down the street. You can't go up and shake hands with him, or get an answer to a question you forgot to ask him at the past time you are remembering. In other words, you are not looking at the actual past at all. You are looking at a present trace of the past. . . . From memories you infer that there have been past events. But you are not aware of any past events. You know the past only in the present and as part of the present."

Thus, I never know the actual past at all, I know only memories of the past, and those memories exist only as a present experience. Further, when what we call the "past" actually occurred, it was a present occurrence. *At no point, therefore, am I ever directly aware of an actual past.* In the same way, I never know the future, I know only anticipations or expectations—which nevertheless are themselves parts of present experience. Anticipation, like memory, is a present fact.

To see that the past as memory and the future as anticipation are both present facts is to see all time existing now. With this understanding, the sayings of the mystics on time and eternity become much clearer. For instance, read Meister Eckhart's famous statement on the two types of biblical days: "There are more days than one. There is the soul's day and God's day. A day, whether six or seven ago, or more than six thousand years ago, is just as near to the present as yesterday. Why? Because all time is contained in the present Now-moment. The soul's day falls within this time and consists of the natural light in which things are seen. God's day, however, is the complete day, comprising both day and night. It is the real Now-moment. The past and future are both far from God and alien from his way." Or Nicholas de Cusa: "All temporal succession coincides in one and the same Eternal Now. So there is nothing past or future." And we can understand why Dante could speak of that incredible "Moment to which all times are present."

So it is that our bondage to time and all its problems is a vast illusion. There is no time but now, and the only thing you ever experience is the eternal present—whatever its outward forms may be. But most of us usually feel that *our* present moment is hardly an eternal one. We feel instead that our present moment is a slender present, a fleeting present lasting about one, maybe two, seconds. This is what the Christian mystics call the *nunc fluens,* which means the "passing present." Another way to say this is that we feel our present moment is *bounded* and *limited.* It seems to be sandwiched in between the past and the future. For, through the confusion of memory-symbols with fact, we impose a *boundary* upon the timeless present, severing it into the opposites of past vs. future, and then conceive of time as a movement from the past through our "fleeting present" to the future. We introduce a boundary into the territory of eternity and thereby fence ourselves in.

Our passing present, then, seems bounded on the one side by the past and on the other by the future. The past seems to be something real and substantial *behind* me, something real that I look backward to. Many people feel that the past lies not only behind them, but to their "left," probably because we read from left to right. At any rate, because we imagine memory to point to a real past, that "past" appears to lie behind our present. It therefore *limits* our present, and seems to stand against it from behind, from the left, from outside.

On the other side of our passing present lies the future. It, too, seems very real and substantial—a little more uncertain than the past, of course, because we can only guess what it will be like. But *that* it is there seems certain. The future bounds our present in the front, ahead of us, to the right of us. Because we imagine expectation to point to a real future, that future seems to lie in front of my present. It therefore bounds my present.

From all sides, then, our present is bounded, sandwiched in between past and future. It is limited, fenced, restricted. It is not an open moment; it is a squeezed moment, a pressed moment, and therefore a fleeting moment. It just passes. Since the past and the future seem so real, our present moment, the very meat of the sandwich, is reduced to a mere thin slice, so that our reality soon becomes all bread-ends with no filling.

But when it is seen that the past as memory is always a present experience, the boundary *behind* this moment collapses. It becomes obvious that nothing came before this present. And likewise, when it is seen that the future of expectation is always a present experience, the boundary *ahead* of this moment explodes. The whole weight of there being something behind us or in front of us quickly, suddenly, and completely vanishes. This present is no longer hemmed in, but expands to fill all time, and thus the "passing present" unfolds into the eternal present, which the Christian mystics call the *nunc stans.* The *nunc fluens,* or passing present, returns to the *nunc stans,* or eternal present. And *this* present is no mere slice of reality. On the contrary, in this now resides the cosmos, with all the time and the space in the world.

This now, the *nunc stans,* is a no-boundary moment. It has no boundaries because the past as memory and the future as expectation are *in* it, not around it. Because there is no past and no future *outside* this now-moment, there are no boundaries to this moment—nothing came before it, nothing comes after it. You never experience a beginning to it; you never experience an end to it. Says the *Platform Sutra:*

> In this moment there is nothing which comes to be. In this moment there is nothing which ceases to be. Thus there is no birth-and-death to be brought to an end. Thus the absolute peace in this present moment. Though it is at this moment, there is no boundary or limit to this moment, and herein is eternal delight.

Thus, it is not true that the mystics flee time by keeping their nose glued to the immediate present, thereby shirking their responsibilities in the pressing world of history. If this charge were true, then the mystics would be interested only in the fleeting present, the one- or two-second *nunc fluens.* But they are not. Their awareness floats instead in the eternal present, the *nunc stans.* They do not so much flee time as embrace all time; they are perfectly free to ponder the past and the future, but through the realization that these ponderings, too, are but present events, they are never *bound* by the past and future. The past as memory does not push them, and the future as expectation does not pull them. For this present includes past and future and thus has nothing outside it which can exert a push or a pull. They are not in time at all, for all time is in them.

Finally, we might ask, what has the eternal now, the *nunc stans,* to do with unity consciousness? Is there any relation between them? The answer is that there is no relation between them because they are one and the same thing. As Aldous Huxley put it, "The eternal now *is* a consciousness." As we are referring to it, a unity consciousness.

Unity consciousness lives as the realization that one's true self is no-boundary, embracing the cosmos as a mirror its objects. As we saw in the last chapter, the major apparent obstacle to unity consciousness is the primary boundary, which leads us to erroneously identify ourselves with only the "small self" in here which, we fancy, *has* experiences of the world out there. However, as Krishnamurti has so often pointed out, the separate self, the "little man within," is *composed entirely of memories*. That is, what you now feel to be the inner observer reading this page is nothing but a complex of past memories. Your likes and dislikes, your hopes and fears, your ideas and principles—all are based on memories. As soon as someone asks, "Who are you? Tell me about yourself," you will begin to search your memory for pertinent facts of what you have done, seen, felt, or accomplished in the past. Indeed, claims Krishnamurti, the very feeling that you now exist as a separate entity is itself based entirely on memory. If you get a good grip on yourself, you are holding nothing but a memory.

Of course, Krishnamurti adds, there is nothing whatsoever wrong with remembering the past, for that is essential in this world. Problematic, however, is the fact that we identify with these memories as if they existed outside or apart from the now-moment; that is, as if they embodied a knowledge of an actual outside past.

But look what this means. Because we believe that memory stands *outside* present experience, the memory-self likewise seems to stand *outside* present experience. The self then seems to *have* present experiences instead of *being* present experiences. The feeling that memory is a past experience *behind* the present moment is the very same feeling as the self being a separate entity *behind* present experience. The observer seems to stand outside Now only because memory seems to actually be a past experience. The observer is memory; if memory seems different from the Now, then the observer feels different from the Now.

Yet, by the same token, when all memory is understood and seen to be a present experience, then the basis of a self standing apart from the present totally collapses. Your "self," which is just memory, thus becomes only another present experience—it is not something which *has* a present experience. As the past merges into the present, you as observer likewise merge into the present. You can no longer stand aside from this moment, for there is no place outside this moment.

Thus, to see all memory as present experience is to collapse the boundaries of this present moment, to free it of illusory limits, to deliver it from the opposites of past vs. future. It becomes obvious that there is nothing behind you in time nor before you in time. You thus have nowhere to stand but in the timeless present, and thus nowhere to stand but in eternity.

6

The Growth of Boundaries

WE HAVE SPENT a rather long time on the nature of timeless unity consciousness, for once this no-boundary awareness is understood, even in the most general terms, then the nature of the rest of the spectrum of consciousness becomes much clearer. Orthodox psychology, in defining a person's real self as ego, has to describe unity consciousness as a breakdown of normality, as an aberration of consciousness, or as an altered state of consciousness. But once unity consciousness is seen as a person's natural self, the only real self, then the ego may be understood as an unnatural restriction and constriction of unity consciousness. Indeed, every level of the spectrum can be understood as a progressive *bounding,* or limiting, or constricting of one's real self, of unity consciousness and no-boundary awareness.

In this chapter we will be looking at this remarkable story of the growth of boundaries. Nature, we have seen, knows nothing of this crazy world of boundaries—there are no walls or fences in nature. Yet we seem to live almost completely within a world of boundaries, a world of walls and limits, bounds and battles. Since our only real self is always unity consciousness, how is it that the other levels of consciousness seem to exist? What happens to give rise to all these various levels of identity?

Since every level of the spectrum is a progressive bounding and limiting of unity consciousness, we need only begin our study of the growth of the boundaries at the very beginning, at the first cause, at the first boundary itself. And we have seen this first boundary before. We called it the primary boundary: that split between the seer and the seen, the knower and the known, the subject and the object. And once this primary boundary occurs, a chain of inevitable consequences follows. A host of other boundaries ensue, each being built upon its predecessor; the various levels of the spectrum exfoliate; the world as we collectively know it leaps into existence; and we becomes lost, amazed and enchanted, distracted and complexed, loving and loathing our universe of opposites.

Religion, philosophy, mythology, and even science have offered accounts of this beginning, this first cause, this impulse to creation itself. Astronomers tell us that approximately 15 billion years ago there was nothing, absolutely and completely nothing, and then. . . . Bang! Out of zero, a magnificent explosion which flung existence into the cosmos. Christian mythology tells that thousands of years ago, there was only God, and then, in a series of six-day mini-bangs, the world as we know it came to be. From science with its Big Bang to religion with its Big Daddy, all have sought to pinpoint this initial movement of creation and manifestation. But search as they might in the past, they will never find a satisfactory solution to this first cause, and for the sufficient reason that the past doesn't exist. This first cause did not occur yesterday. Rather, it is a present occurrence, a present fact, a present activity. Furthermore, this first cause is not to be ascribed to a God apart from our being, for God is the real self of all that is. The primary boundary, this perpetually active first cause, is our doing in *this* moment.

The most puzzling aspect of all this is *why* the primary boundary arises at all. Why, to put it in a different form, original sin? Why a world of samsara, maya, the misery of boundaries? This is the natural question to ask, and yet it is a booby-trapped puzzle. For when we ask, "Why the primary boundary?," we are really asking what came before the primary boundary. But nothing precedes the primary boundary. That is, nothing causes it, nothing produces it, nothing brings it into existence. If there were a cause to the primary boundary, then that cause would itself be the new primary boundary. In theological terms, if the first cause had a cause, it wouldn't be the *first* cause. And so, unsatisfactory as it initially seems, the only possible answer to the question, "Why the primary boundary?," is that there is no why. Rather, the primary boundary arises of itself, as one's own present activity, but as an activity which is itself uncaused. It is a movement in and by one's unity consciousness, a movement that has many results, but is not itself a result.

We will return to this initial movement in the last chapter, and see if we can penetrate its secret activity, but all we can say at this point is that suddenly in this moment, and in this moment, and in this moment again the primary boundary arises. We have seen—as in the concave-convex example—that each time a boundary is superimposed upon reality, that boundary generates two apparently contradictory opposites. And the same thing occurs with the primary boundary. For the primary boundary severs unity consciousness itself, splitting it right down the middle and delivering it up as a subject vs. an object, as a knower vs. a known, as a seer vs. a seen, or in more earthy terms, as an organism vs. an environment. The natural *line*—the skin-line which is not to be denied—between the organism and the environment becomes an illusory boundary, a fence, a separation of that which is really inseparable. Says Krishnamurti, "And in that distance, the division between the seer and the thing seen, in that division the whole conflict of man exists."

Notice that when this primary boundary occurs (and it is occurring now, moment to moment), then man is no longer identified with his organism *and* his environment, he is no longer one with the world he perceives, because these two "opposites" now seem irreconcilable. He is identified instead with *only* his organism as *against* his environment. The organism is "self," but the entire environment is "not-self." He takes up residence on *this* side of the skin boundary, and stares out and across to the alien world around him. "I, a stranger, alone, afraid, in a world I never made." With the primary boundary, man forgets his prior identity with the All and concentrates it exclusively on his bodymind.

Thus it comes about that man pretends to leave his real self, pretends to leave the level of unity consciousness, and imagines that he lives only as a separate and isolated organism. But this is precisely the *creation* of the next major level of the spectrum—namely, the level of the total organism. So the primary boundary severs the unity of the organism-environment, and creates the apparently conflicting opposites of organism versus environment, me in here versus the world out there. All subsequent boundaries will rest upon this initial foundation, for, as Chuang Tzu explained, "If there is no other, there will be no self. If there is no self, there will be none to make distinctions."

With the primary boundary, our now separate self appears set apart, forever apart, by an unbridgeable gulf from the world "around" it. We no longer are the world, we face it. Unity consciousness becomes individual consciousness, our Supreme Identity becomes a personal identity, the Self becomes a self. And thus the first two major opposites, the subject-seer and object-seen, are torn apart from their eternal embrace and now face each other as mortal enemies. So begins the battle of me vs.

my world. The environment out there has become a potential threat, since it has the power to eradicate what I now feel to be my "real" self, namely, my organism, my bodymind. Thus there appears, for the very first time, an entirely new factor, a factor destined to be of overwhelming significance: there now appears the conscious fear of death.

An old Taoist sage said, "The True Individuals of old knew nothing of the love of life or of the hatred of death. Entrance into life occasioned them no joy; exit from it awakened no resistance. Composedly they went and came. Thus there was in them the want of any mind to resist the Tao, and of all attempts by means of the human to resist the Heavenly." But what kind of individual is a True Individual? Elsewhere the same sage speaks of a True Individual thus: "I am not attached to the body and I give up any idea of knowing. By freeing myself from the body and mind [i.e., the separate organism or bodymind], I become one with the infinite." In other words, death of the organism is only a problem to a self which identifies exclusively with that organism.

For at the moment an individual separates her "self" from the environment, then and only then does this conscious fear of death arise. The True Individuals of old didn't fear death, not because they were too stupid to know any better, but because, "transcending the body and mind," they were eternally one with the infinite. And the True Individual, as Rinzai would point out, is really one's own True Self, one's own unity consciousness. When a person realizes that her fundamental self is the self of the cosmos, then the apparent death of individual forms is not only acceptable but willed.

And I laid me down with a will.

Only parts face death, not the Whole. But as soon as a person imagines the real self to be *exclusively* confined to a particular organism, then concern with the death of *that* organism becomes all-consuming. The problem of death, the fear of nothingness, becomes the core of the self which imagines it is only a part.

This primal mood of fear also makes it nearly impossible for the separate self to understand and accept the oneness of life and death. Like *all* the other opposites we have examined, being and nonbeing form an inseparable unity. Behind their apparent difference, they are each other. Living and dying, birth and death, are simply two different ways of viewing *this* timeless moment.

Look at it this way: Anything which is just born, which has just come into existence, has no past behind it. Birth, in other words, is the condition of *having no past*. And likewise, anything which now dies, which has just ceased to be, has no future left in front of it. Death is the condition of *having no future*. But we have already seen that this present moment has *both* no past *and* no future simultaneously. That is, birth and death are *one* in this present moment. This moment is just now being born—you can never find a past to this present moment, you can never find something before it. Yet also, this moment is just now dying—you can never find a future to this moment, never find something after it. This present, then, is a coincidence of opposites, a unity of birth and death, being and non-being, living and dying. As Ippen put it, "Every moment is the last moment and every moment is a rebirth."

But man, in identifying exclusively with his organism (the primary boundary), accepts only *half* of birth-and-death. The death half is refused. Death, in fact, is precisely what he now fears above all else. And since death is the condition of having no future, when man refuses death, that really means that he *refuses to live without a future*. In fact, man demands a future as a promise that he will not so much as smell death in this present moment. His fear of death, whether operating overtly or subtly, propels him always to think, plan, yearn, or at least intend for tomorrow. His fear of death causes him to search for a future, reach out for a future, and move toward a future. In short, his fear of death generates in him an intense sensation of *time*. Ironically, because the separate self is an illusion, the actual death of the separate self is also an illusion. As the Sufi mystic Hazrat Inayat Khan put it, "There is no such thing as mortality, except the illusion, and the impression of that illusion, which man keeps before himself as fear during his lifetime." At this level, man creates the illusion of time so as to assuage his fear of an illusory death.

In this sense, time is an illusion pushing against an illusion. There is a story about a man who met an old and rather feeble-looking fellow on a bus trip. The old man had a brown paper sack in one hand, and he was placing bits of food into it. Finally the passenger could stand it no longer, and asked what was in the paper sack he was feeding? "It's a mongoose. You know, the animal that can kill snakes." "But why do you carry it with you?" "Well," the old man replied, "I'm an alcoholic, and I need the mongoose to frighten off the snakes when I get the delirium tremens." "But don't you know that the snakes are just imaginary?" "Oh sure," the old man replied, "but so is the mongoose." Likewise, we use the illusion of time to frighten off the illusion of death.

The eternal and timeless now is an awareness that knows neither past nor future. The eternal now has no future, no boundary, no tomorrow—nothing ahead of it, nothing in front of it, nothing after it. But that is also the very *condition* of death, for death is the state of having no future, no tomorrow, no time to come. To accept death is thus to be totally comfortable living without a future, that is, living in the present above time, as Emerson put it.

But with the rise of the primary boundary, man refuses death, and therefore refuses to live without a future. Man refuses, in short, to live without time. He demands time, creates time, lives in time. Survival becomes his hope, time becomes his most precious possession, the future becomes his only goal. Time, the ultimate source of all his problems, thus becomes the imagined source of his salvation. He rushes into time . . . until his time comes, and he is faced, as he was in the beginning, with the core of this own separate self—and it is death.

> Tomorrow, and tomorrow, and tomorrow,
> Creeps in this petty pace from day to day
> To the last syllable of recorded time,
> And all our yesterdays have lighted fools
> The way to dusty death.

Because we demand a future, we live each moment in expectation and unfulfillment. We live each moment *in passing*. In just this way the real *nunc stans,* the timeless present, is reduced to the *nunc fluens,* the fleeting present, the passing present of a mere one or two seconds. We expect each moment *to pass* on to a future moment, for in this fashion we pretend to avoid death by always rushing toward an imagined future. We want to meet ourselves in the future. We don't want just now—we want another now, and another, and another, tomorrow and tomorrow and tomorrow. And thus, paradoxically, our impoverished present is fleeting precisely because we demand that it end! We want it to end so that it can thereby pass on to yet another moment, a future moment, which will in turn live only to pass.

Yet this is only half the story of time. Because man is now identified solely with his organism, the memory traces naturally present in that organism assume a significance out of all proper proportion and become his consuming preoccupation. He clings to his memory as if it were real—which is to say, as if it reported a real past of a real self. He becomes quietly obsessed with his "past"; he identifies with it unconditionally. Because he demands a real future *ahead* of him, he likes to see a real past *behind* him, and this he engineers by pretending that memory gives a knowledge of actual past events instead of being part of his present experience. He clings to memory as a promise that he once existed yesterday and therefore will likely exist tomorrow. He thus lives only in memory and expectation, bounding and limiting his present with bittersweet laments of time past and poignant hopes of time to come. He wants something around his present to protect him from death, and so he bounds it with the past and the future.

Notice, with reference to figure 1 (on page 441), that man is now identified with his total organism as it exists in space and time. (I should point out that the large diagonal slash line represents the self/not-self boundary, whose changes we are following. We have just seen it shift from the universe to the individual organism.) So far, however, we have omitted any discussion of the intermediate levels of the transpersonal bands. These bands are too subtle and complicated to discuss at this point. We will return to them in chapter 9, for by that time we will have the necessary background information to make some sense out of them. For now we need only note that these are the bands of only the spectrum where, as suggested diagrammatically in figure 1, the individual's identity is not quite with the All (which would be the level of unity consciousness), but then neither is it confined to the isolated bodymind (which would be the level of the total organism). At these bands, the self/not-self boundary expands in a very positive sense, so that one finds here a level of awareness that clearly transcends the separate organism.

Let us return to the level of the total organism and continue with the story of the growth of the spectrum. At this level, the individual is identified solely with her organism, existing in time, in flight from death. Nevertheless, she is at least still in touch with her entire psychophysical being. This is why we usually refer to the level of the total organism by a simpler name: the centaur. A centaur is a legendary animal, half human and half horse, and so it well represents a perfect union and harmony of mental and physical. A centaur is not a horse rider in control of her horse, but a rider who is one with her horse. Not a psyche divorced from and in control of a soma, but a self-controlling, self-governing, psychosomatic unity.

But now we come to a major event. With the rise of the next level of the spectrum—the ego level—the centaur is literally broken. For the individual refuses to remain in touch with all of her organism; she refuses to extend her identity to all her organic activities; she refuses globally to feel herself. Instead, she narrows her identity to only a facet of her total organism. She identifies exclusively with her ego, her self-image, her purely mental personality, the abstract portion of the centaur. And this means she denies the body and rejects it on a fundamental level by turning it into property. She is the rider, the controller—and the body is reduced to the role of stupid beast, the ridden, the controlled, the horse.

Why does this occur? Why this new addition of yet another boundary? What pushes the individual away from her centaur, her total organism? As one might expect, there are several reasons for this new boundary between mind and body, but an outstanding one is that the individual is still in flight from death. She avoids everything that might remind her of death, embody death, or even hint at death. And as she constructs her reality in flight from death, the first and most problematic thing she encounters is: her body. The body seems to be the ultimate home of death. She knows her body is mortal; she knows it will decay and rot out from under her. In an uncompromising way, the body is impermanent; and the individual, in flight from death, seeks only that which will promise her a tomorrow—in truth, an immortality of tomorrows. And that plainly leaves the body out.

Thus man comes to nurse the secret desire that his self should be permanent, static, unchanging, imperturbable, everlasting. But this is just what symbols, concepts, and ideas are like. They are static, unmoving, unchanging, and fixed. The word "tree," for example, remains the same word even though every real tree changes, grows, transforms, and dies. Seeking this static immortality, man therefore begins to center his identity around an *idea* of himself—and this is the mental abstraction called the "ego." Man will not live with his body, for that is corruptible, and thus he lives only as his ego, a picture of himself to himself, and a picture that leaves out any true reference to death.

Thus is the ego level born (see figure 1). The natural line between the mind and body becomes an illusory boundary, a fortified fence, an armed wall separating that which is really inseparable. And since each boundary carries a new battle, a new war of opposites is on. The desires of the flesh are pitted against the wants of the soul, and all too often the "spirit is willing but the flesh is weak." The organism becomes divided against itself, forsaking thereby its deeper integrity. Man loses touch with his total organism, and the most he will allow is a mental representation, a self-image, of that total organism. It is not exactly that man loses touch with his body. Rather, he loses touch with the *unity* of the body and mind, the unity of feeling and attention that is characteristic of the centaur. The whole clarity of feeling-attention becomes disrupted and distorted, and in its place is left compulsive thinking on the one hand, and the dissociated body on the other.

Thus we find ourselves on the ego level: man identified with a mental reflection of his total organism, with a self-image. Now a more or less accurate self-image is a loose self-image. It makes room for the entire conventional history of the organism. It includes the childish aspects of the organism, the emotional aspects, the rational as well as the irrational. It knows the strengths and weaknesses of the entire organism. It possesses a conscience (or "superego"), a bittersweet gift from the parents, and a philosophic outlook, which is a personal matrix of boundaries. A healthy ego integrates and harmonizes all these various aspects.

Occasionally, however, all is not well within the ego. For uncertain circumstances, an individual can refuse to touch aspects of his own ego. Some of the ego's wishes and desires seem so strange, threatening, or taboo that a person will refuse to acknowledge them. He fears that to *have* a wish is the same as to *act* on that wish, and that would bring such terrible consequences that he simply denies that he has the wish in the first place.

He might, for example, have a fleeting wish, a minor aspect of his egoic tendencies, to attack someone. Few people escape these temporary wishes. But afraid that he might *act* on that wish, he simply denies ownership of it—and then forgets that he denied it. "Me? I'd never even think of such a thing. And since I wouldn't, there's just no need for me to deny it in the first place." But, alas, the wish does remain his, and he can only pretend to disown it. As regards the self/not-self boundary, the taboo wish goes on the *other* side, or at least appears to. In similar fashion, all of the facets of the ego which are disliked, or not understood and accepted, are secretly placed on the opposite side of the fence. And there they join the enemy's forces.

To illustrate this split within the ego, take the fellow just mentioned who wishes to attack someone (say his boss), but instead denies awareness of that wish. The wish does not thereby evaporate. It still exists, but it seems to exist *outside* the ego. In technical jargon, the wish is projected. The guy knows somebody is fighting mad, but since it obviously isn't him, he has to pick a candidate. The angry impulse, in other words, is still present and still active, but since he denies that it is his, he can find it in the only other place possible: in other people. Suddenly, people in the environment seem to be mad at him, and for no apparent reason! His wish to fight now appears to come *from* others and to be aimed *at* him, instead of the other way around. "I'm mad at the world," when projected, becomes "The world is mad at me." He understandably develops symptoms of depression.

But something else significant has happened. For the person is now no longer in touch with all of his egoic tendencies. Not only can he not *touch* his total organism (the fate of all egos by definition), he can't even *think* about all of his organism's potentials, because some thoughts are now outlawed. He cannot find, in other words, an accurate and acceptable self-image. He has distorted his self-image in an attempt to make it more acceptable, and thus ended up by denying facets of himself. He develops a fraudulent picture of himself, an inaccurate self-image. He develops, in short, a *persona,* and all of the unacceptable aspects of his ego now appear as external, foreign, and not-self. They are projected as the *shadow.* A boundary is erected within the ego, and the individual's sense of self narrows as a consequence—while his sense of menacing not-self grows. Thus develops the persona level (see figure 1).

And so we see that through successive boundaries, the spectrum of consciousness evolves. Each time a new boundary is drawn, the person's sense of self diminishes, shrinks, becomes less roomy, more narrowed and restricted. First the environment, then the body, then the shadow appear as not-self, as "existing out there," as being foreign objects, and enemy objects at that, for every boundary line is a battle line.

But all of these "objects out there" are just *projections* of a person's own being, and they all can be rediscovered as aspects of one's own self. It is this process of discovery that we will undertake in the rest of this book. And each discovery, though sometimes painful, is finally a joy, for each discovery that an object out there is really an aspect of one's own self converts enemies into friends, wars into dances, battles into plays. The shadow, the body, and the entire environment have become part of our unconscious, the consequence of our fantasy dreams in a world of maps and boundaries, the gift of Adam to his sleeping sons and daughters. Let us, then, lift the boundaries and look afresh at the real world. Let us lift the boundaries so that we can once again touch our shadows, our bodies, and our world, knowing too that all we touch is at heart the original face of our own true self.

7

The Persona Level

THE START OF DISCOVERY

THE MOVEMENT of descent and discovery begins at the moment you consciously become dissatisfied with life. Contrary to most professional opinion, this gnawing dissatisfaction with life is not a sign of "mental illness," nor an indication of poor social adjustment, nor a character disorder. For concealed within this basic unhappiness with life and existence is the embryo of a growing intelligence, a special intelligence usually buried under the immense weight of social shams. A person who is beginning to sense the suffering of life is, at the same time, beginning to *awaken* to deeper realities, truer realities. For suffering smashes to pieces the complacency of our normal fictions about reality, and forces us to become alive in a special sense—to see carefully, to feel deeply, to touch ourselves and our worlds in ways we have heretofore avoided. It has been said, and truly I think, that suffering is the first grace. In a special sense, suffering is almost a time of rejoicing, for it marks the birth of creative insight.

But only in a special sense. Some people cling to their suffering as a mother to its child, carrying it as a burden they dare not set down. They do not face suffering with awareness, but rather clutch at their suffering, secretly transfixed with the spasms of martyrdom. Suffering should neither be denied awareness, avoided, despised, not glorified, clung to, dramatized. The emergence of suffering is not so much good as it is a good sign, an indication that one is starting to realize that life lived outside unity consciousness is ultimately painful, distressing, and sorrowful. The life of boundaries is a life of battles—of fear, anxiety, pain, and finally death. It is only through all manner of numbing compensations, distractions, and enchantments that we agree not to question our illusory boundaries, the root cause of the endless wheel of agony. But sooner or later, if we are not rendered totally insensitive, our defensive compensations begin to fail their soothing and concealing purpose. As a consequence, we begin to suffer in one way or another, because our awareness is finally directed toward the conflict-ridden nature of our false boundaries and the fragmented life supported by them.

Suffering, then, is the initial movement of the recognition of false boundaries. Correctly understood, it is therefore liberating, for it points beyond boundaries altogether. We suffer, then, not because we are sick, but because intelligent insight is emerging. The correct understanding of suffering, however, is necessary in order that the birth of insight is not aborted. We must correctly interpret suffering in order to enter into it, live it, and finally live beyond it. If we do not correctly understand suffering, we simply get stuck in the middle of it—we wallow in it, not knowing what else to do.

Throughout humankind's history, various shamans, priests, sages, mystics, saints, psychologists, and psychiatrists have tried to point out the best ways to live suffering correctly so as to live beyond it. They have confronted men and women with insights into their suffering so that, correctly understanding their suffering, they might go beyond it in freedom. But the insights offered by the various doctors of the soul have not always been of the same nature. In fact, these insights often drastically contradict each other. The more ancient soul doctors advised us to contact God. The modern soul doctors advise us to contact our unconscious. The avant-garde soul doctors advise us to touch our bodies. The clairvoyant soul doctors advise us to transcend our bodies. Today, more than ever before, our doctors of the soul are in strident disagreement, and as a general result we are paralyzed in the middle of our suffering, confused as to what it means, confused even about whom to ask what it means. Frozen in our suffering, our deeper insights into reality do not and cannot emerge. We cannot enter our suffering with awareness so as to liberate the insights hidden in it.

We cannot endure our suffering with fruitful results unless we know what it *means, why* it is occurring. And we don't know what it means because we have no doctor of the soul whom we can truly and completely trust. There was a time when we looked with innocent faith to a priest or sage or shaman as a soul doctor, and he or she aimed our awareness toward God. In the last century, however, the priest was largely displaced by the psychiatrist as the authority to trust if one were really troubled, and this new priest aimed your awareness instead toward aspects of your own psyche. Yet today trust in the psychiatrist is slowly diminishing as a widely respected soul doctor. More modern, effective, and liberating therapies are emerging. Our new doctors of the soul spring out of Esalen and Oasis and similar growth centers across the country, and they are revolutionizing the meaning of "therapy" by directing our awareness to the entire organism and not just the disembodied psyche. We even see developing now the transpersonal soul doctor, who aims our awareness directly at supra-individual consciousness. But, alas, since none of these doctors really agree with one another, whom does one believe?

One of the greatest problems with this general "who's right?" controversy is that laypeople and professionals alike persistently tend to assume that these various soul doctors are approaching the human being from different angles. But they are not. Rather they are approaching *different levels* of human awareness from different angles. Today we have no doctors of the soul whom we can wholeheartedly trust because we imagine they are all speaking about the *same level* of our consciousness. They therefore seem to definitely contradict each other, at least in essentials, and we are caught in the contradiction.

Yet once we recognize the multi-leveled nature of human consciousness, once we understand that our being has many layers, then we can start to see that the various types of therapies are indeed different precisely because they are addressing these different layers of the soul. Thus, if we comprehend that the various soul doctors are validly addressing different levels of consciousness, we may be able to listen more openly to what any particular one has to say about his or her own special level. And if we are suffering on *that* level, we can listen attentively to what they might tell us. They will then likely help us see the meaning of our particular type of suffering, help us endure it with awareness and understanding and insight, and thus help us live beyond it.

Once we become generally familiar with the spectrum of consciousness, with the various layers of our own being, we may more readily spot the level on which we now live as well as the level from which our present suffering, if any, springs. Thus, we will be able to select an appropriate type of soul doctor, an appropriate approach to our present suffering, and thus no longer remain frozen in its midst.

Toward this end, we will in the following chapters be examining some of the major levels of the spectrum. We'll look at the different potentials and joys and values inherent in each level, and particularly the different dis-eases, pains, and symptoms which arise from each level. We'll also examine the major "therapies" which have evolved to deal with the particular sufferings which spring from the various levels. Overall this will, I trust, give readers a simple map of the depths of awareness, a map which might help guide them through the amazement of their own boundaries.

We will be working our way back down the spectrum of consciousness. This descent can be usefully described in all sorts of ways, from harmonizing opposites to "expanding" consciousness to transcending complexes, but most fundamentally this descent is a simple dissolving of boundaries. We have seen that each time a new boundary is constructed, we limit, restrict, and narrow our sense of self, so that our prior identity progressively shifts from the universe to the organism to the ego to the persona. In a figurative sense, the self becomes smaller and smaller while the not-self becomes larger and larger. With each boundary a new facet of the self is *projected* and thus appears external, alien, foreign, out there, on the other side of the fence. To construct a particular boundary is therefore to create a particular projection—some facet of self which now appears to be not-self. And likewise, to re-own a projection is to dissolve a boundary. When you realize that a projection which appeared to exist "out there" is really your own reflection, is actually part of yourself, then you have torn down that particular boundary between self and not-self. Hence the field of your awareness becomes that much more expansive, open, free, and undefended. To truly befriend and ultimately become one with a former "enemy" is the same as tearing down the battle line and expanding the territory through which you may freely move. These projected facets will then no longer threaten you because they *are* you. To descend the spectrum, then, is to (1) dissolve a boundary by (2) re-owning a projection. This occurs at each step of the descent.

Most of the ideas on boundary, projection, and the conflict of opposites will become clearer as we proceed with concrete examples. This chapter will be devoted to an understanding of the persona and shadow, as well as the disciplines which have helped people descend from the persona level to the ego level. In the next chapter, we will look at the descent from the ego to the centaur level; in the one after that, from the centaur to the transpersonal; and finally the descent to unity consciousness. Each chapter is basically pragmatic, designed to give the reader (1) a general understanding of the particular level, (2) an experiential taste of that level, and (3) an introduction to the types of "therapies" available today which address that level. These chapters are not designed to actually install one on a particular level, but merely to offer a glimpse of what the therapies on that level are like. To live continuously on one of the deeper levels of consciousness requires a fair amount of work and study. I have therefore included, at the end of each chapter, a list of recommended readings and therapies that deal with that level.

Let us begin where most people find themselves—trapped in the persona. The persona is a more or less inaccurate and impoverished self-image. It is created when the individual attempts to deny to herself the existence of certain of her own tendencies, such as anger, assertiveness, erotic impulses, joy, hostility, courage, aggression, drive, interest, and so on. But as much as she may try to deny these tendencies, they don't thereby vanish. Since these tendencies *are* the individual's, all she can do is pretend that they belong to someone else. Anybody else, as a matter of fact, just not her. So she does not succeed in really denying these tendencies, but only in denying ownership of them. She thus comes to actually believe that these tendencies are not-self, alien, outside. She has *narrowed* her boundaries so as to exclude the unwanted tendencies. These alienated tendencies are therefore projected as the shadow, and the individual is identified only with what's left: a narrowed, impoverished, and inaccurate self-image, the persona. A new boundary is constructed, and another battle of opposites is on: the persona vs. its own shadow.

The essence of shadow projection is simple to comprehend but difficult to undo, because it throttles some of our dearest illusions. Nevertheless, we can see how uncomplicated the process itself actually is from the following example.

Jack wants very much to clean out his garage, which is a total and complete mess; besides, he's been wanting and meaning to clean it for some time. Finally, he decides that now is the perfect time to get the job done, and after climbing into his old work clothes, he heads off with mild enthusiasm to tackle the garage. Now at this point Jack is very much in touch with his own *drive,* because he knows that despite the work involved this is definitely something he *wants* to do. True, part of him doesn't want to clean up the mess, but the important fact is that *his desire to clean the garage is greater than his desire not to clean it,* or he wouldn't be doing it in the first place.

But a strange thing begins to happen as Jack arrives on the scene and surveys the incredible mess lying where his garage should be. He starts to have second thoughts about the whole matter. But he doesn't leave. Instead he putters around, reads all the old magazines, plays with his old catcher's mitt, daydreams, fidgets about. At this point, Jack is starting to lose touch with his drive. But again, the important point is that his desire to clean the garage is still present, because if it weren't he would simply leave the job and do something else. He doesn't leave the job because his desire to do it is still greater than his desire not to. But he is starting to forget his own drive, and therefore he will start to alienate and project it.

The projection of his drive works like this: Jack's desire to clean the garage is, as we have seen, still present. It is therefore still active and so it constantly clamors for attention, just as hunger, for example, will constantly demand that you act upon that drive by eating something. Because the drive to clean the garage is still present and active, Jack knows, in the back of his mind, that *somebody* wants him to clean the garage. And that's precisely why he is still puttering around in it. Jack knows that somebody wants him to clean up, but his problem is that at this point he has forgotten *who* it is. Thus he starts to get angry and annoyed with the whole project, and as the hours drag on, he gets more and more upset with his plight. All he really needs to complete the projection—that is, to totally forget his *own* drive to clean the garage—is a likely candidate on whom he can "hang" his own projected drive. Since he knows somebody is pushing him to clean up, and that is annoying the daylights out of him, he'd really like to find the "other" person who is pushing him.

Enter the unsuspecting victim: Jack's wife happens by the garage, pokes her head in, and innocently asks if he has finished cleaning up. In a mild fit, Jack snaps that she should "get off his back!" For he now feels that not *he* but his *wife* wants him to clean the garage. The projection is completed, for Jack's own drive now appears to come from the outside. He has projected it, put it on the other side of the fence, and from there it seems to attack him.

Jack starts to feel, therefore, that his wife is *pressuring* him. Yet the only thing he is actually feeling is his own projected drive, his own misplaced desire to clean the garage. Jack might yell at his wife that he doesn't want to clean the stupid garage at all, and that she is just nagging and pressuring him. But if Jack really did not want to clean the garage, if he were really innocent of that drive, he would have simply answered that he had changed his mind and would clean it some other day. But he did not, because in the back of his mind he knew that *somebody* really wanted that garage cleaned, but since it "wasn't" him, it had to be someone else. The wife, of course, is a likely candidate; and as she enters the scene, Jack throws his projected drive onto her.

In short, Jack projected his own drive and therefore experienced it as *external drive,* as coming from the outside. Another name for external drive is *pressure.* In fact, anytime a person projects some sort of drive, he will feel pressure, he will feel his own drive coming back at him from the outside. Further—and this is where most people blink in utter disbelief—*all* pressure is the result of projected drive. In this example, notice that if Jack did not possess the drive to clean the garage, he could not have felt any pressure from his wife. He would have felt very calm about the situation and have said he didn't feel like doing it today or that he had changed his mind. Instead he felt pressured! But he did not actually feel his wife pressuring him—he felt his *own* drive pressuring him. No drive, no pressure. All pressure is at bottom a person's own displaced drive.

But what if the wife marched into the garage and actually did demand that Jack clean it? Surely that would change the whole story, would it not? If Jack then felt pressured, wouldn't this be because his wife was pushing him? Wouldn't Jack be feeling her pressure and not his own? Actually, this does not change the story at all. It will just make it much easier for Jack to hang his projection on her. We say she is a good "hook" because she is displaying the *same* tendency which Jack is about to project onto her. This makes it oh-so-inviting for Jack to project his drive onto his wife, but it is still *his* drive. He must have that drive, and he must project it, or there is just no *feeling* of pressure. His wife might indeed be "pressuring" him to do something, but he won't actually *feel* pressure unless he *also* wants to do it and *then* projects it. His feelings are just that—*his* feelings.

Thus, therapists on this level will suggest that the person who feels constantly pressured simply has more drive and energy than he knows. If he didn't have that drive, then he wouldn't care less. The wise individual, then, whenever he feels some sort of pressure—from the boss, from the spouse, from school, friends, associates, or children—learns to use those feelings of pressure as a *signal* that he has some energy and drive that he is presently unaware of. He learns to *translate* "I feel pressured" into "I have more drive than I know." Once he realizes that all feelings of pressure are his own unheeded drive, he can then decide afresh whether to act on his drive, or to postpone acting on his drive. But either way, he finally knows that it is *his* drive.

The basic mechanism of projection itself is thus fairly simple. An impulse (such as drive, anger, or desire) which arises *in* you and is naturally *aimed at* the environment, *when projected,* appears as an impulse originating *in* the environment and aimed *at* you. It's a boomerang effect, and you end up clobbering yourself with your own energy. No longer do you push to action, you feel pushed into action. You have placed the impulse on the other side of the self/not-self boundary, and so naturally it attacks *you* from the outside, instead of helping you attack the environment.

So we can see that there are two major consequences of shadow projection. First, you feel that you completely lack the projected impulse, trait, or tendency. And second, it appears to exist "out there," in the environment, usually in other people. The self is made less and the not-self is made more. But as uncomfortable as this can be, a person who is projecting will vigorously defend his mistaken view of reality. If you approached Jack while he was yelling at his innocent wife and tried to point out that his feelings of being pressured and nagged were really his own drive, you would probably get hit. For it is of the utmost importance that the individual *prove* his projections are really out there threatening him.

At any rate, most people have a very strong *resistance* to accepting their own shadows, a resistance to admitting that their projected impulses and traits *are* theirs. Resistance, as a matter of fact, is a major cause of projection. A person resists his shadow, resists the disliked aspects of himself, and therefore projects them. So wherever there is a projection, there is some sort of resistance lurking close by. Sometimes this resistance is mild, sometimes violent, but nowhere is its operation more plainly evident than in that most common form of projection, the witch hunt.

Almost everybody, at one time or another, has seen, heard, or participated in some form of a witch hunt, and as grotesque as these things can be, they nevertheless illustrate the disasters of projection and the persistent blindness of people to their own foibles. At the same time, the witch hunt offers the very clearest example of the truth of projection, the truth that we loathe in others those things, and only those things, that we secretly loathe in ourselves.

The witch hunt begins when a person loses track of some trait or tendency in herself which he deems evil, satanic, demonic, or at least unworthy. Actually, this tendency or trait could be the most inconsequential thing imaginable—a bit of human perversity, orneriness, or rascality. All of us have a dark side. But "dark side" does not mean "bad side"; it means only that we all have a little black heart ("There's a little bit of larceny in everybody's heart"), which, if we are fairly aware and accepting of it, actually adds much to the spice of life. According to the Hebrew tradition, God himself placed this wayward, whimsical, or perverse tendency in all people at the very beginning, presumably to prevent humankind from perishing from boredom.

But the witch hunter believes that she has no little black heart. She assumes to some degree a peculiar air of righteousness. It isn't that she lacks a little black heart, as she would like to believe and like to have you believe, but that she is extremely uncomfortable with her little black heart. She *resists* it in herself, tries to deny it, attempts to cast it out. But it remains, as it must, and it remains *hers,* persistently clamoring for some attention. The more her little black heart clamors for attention, the more she resists it. The more she resists it, the more strength it acquires, and the more it demands her awareness. Finally, because she can deny it no longer, she does start to see it. But she sees it in the only way she can—as residing in *other* people. She knows *somebody* has a little black heart, but since it just can't be her, it must be someone else. All she has to do now is find this somebody else, and this becomes an extremely important task, because if she can't find someone onto whom she can project her shadow, she will be left holding it herself. It is here that we see the resistance playing its crucial role. For just as the person once hated and resisted her own shadow with unbridled passion, and sought to eradicate it by any means, she now despises, with the very same passion, those onto whom she casts her own shadow.

Sometime the witch hunting takes on atrocious dimensions—the Nazi persecution of Jews, the Salem witch trials, the Ku Klux Klan scapegoating of blacks. Notice, however, that in all such cases the persecutor hates the persecuted for precisely those traits that the persecutor displays with a glaringly uncivilized fury. At other times, the witch hunt appears in less terrifying proportions—the cold war fear of a "Commie under every bed," for instance. And often, it appears in comic form—the interminable gossip about everybody else that tells you much more about the gossiper than about the object of gossip. But all of these are instances of individuals desperate to prove that their own shadows belong to other people.

Many men and women will launch into tirades about how disgusting homosexuals are. Despite how decent and rational they otherwise try to behave, they find themselves seized with a loathing of any homosexual, and in an emotional outrage will advocate such things as suspending gay civil rights (or worse). But why does such an individual hate homosexuals so passionately? Oddly, he doesn't hate the homosexual because he is homosexual; he hates him because he sees in the homosexual what he secretly fears he himself might become. He is most uncomfortable with his own natural, unavoidable, but minor homosexual tendencies, and so projects them. He thus comes to hate the homosexual inclinations in other people—but only because he first hates them in himself.

And so, in one form or another, the witch hunt goes. We hate people "because," we say, they are dirty, stupid, perverted, immoral. . . . They might be exactly what we say they are. Or they might not. That is totally irrelevent, however, because we *hate* them only if we ourselves unknowingly possess the despised traits ascribed to them. We hate them because they are a constant reminder of aspects of ourselves that we are loathe to admit.

We are starting to see an important indicator of projection. Those items in the environment (people or things) that strongly *affect* us instead of just *informing* us are usually our own projections. Items that bother us, upset us, repulse us, or at the other extreme, attract us, compel us, obsess us—these are usually reflections of the shadow. As an old proverb has it,

> I looked, and looked, and this I came to see:
> That what I thought was you and you,
> Was really me and me.

With this basic understanding of the shadow, we can now unravel some other common projections. Thus, just as pressure is projected drive, obligation is projected desire. That is, persistent feelings of obligation are a signal that you are doing something that you don't admit you *want* to do. Feelings of obligation, feelings of "I have to for *your* sake," arise most often in the family situation. The parents feel obligated to take care of the kids, the husband feels obligated to support the wife, the wife feels obligated to accommodate the husband, and so on. People, however, eventually begin to resent obligations, no matter how delightful they may seem to an outsider. As this resentment grows, the individual is likely to revert to witch hunting, and thus he and his spouse usually end up at the witch doctor, commonly called the marriage counselor.

The person who feels he is under terrible obligations to do such-and-such is simply projecting his real desire to do such-and-such. Yet this is exactly what he won't admit (in his resistance to the shadow). In fact, he will tell you precisely the opposite: he will claim that he feels obligated because he really *doesn't* want to do such-and-such. But that can't be quite true, because if he really lacked all desire to help, he wouldn't feel obligated at all. He wouldn't care less! It is not that he doesn't want to help, it's that he wants to and won't admit it. He wants to help others, but projecting this desire, he then feels that *others* want him to help. Thus, obligation is not the weight of demands from others, but the weight of one's own unacknowledged friendliness.

Let's examine another common projection. Perhaps nothing is more painful than the feeling of acute self-consciousness, the feeling that everybody is staring at us. Maybe we have to give a speech, or act in a play, or receive an award, and we freeze because we feel that everybody is looking at us. But many people don't freeze in public. So the problem must lie not in the situation itself but in something we are doing in the situation. And what we are doing, according to many therapists, is projecting our own interest in people, so that *everybody* seems interested in us. Instead of actively looking, we feel looked at. We give our eyes to the audience, so that their natural interest in us seems blown out of proportion into a massive amount of interest zeroed-in on us personally, watching every move, every detail, every action. And so naturally we freeze. And will stay frozen until we dare to take back the projection—to look instead of feeling looked-at, to give attention instead of being clobbered by it.

Along the same line, imagine what might happen if a person projected a bit of hostility, a bit of her desire to aggressively attack the environment. She would feel that people were being unnecessarily hostile and provocative toward her, and she would consequently start to become intimidated, fearful, perhaps even terrified by the amount of hostile energies zeroed-in on her. But this fear would be the result not of the environment, but of her projection of hostility into the environment. Thus, in most cases a person's unrealistic fear of people or places is just a signal, a tip-off, that she is angry and hostile but doesn't know it.

In a similar vein, one of the most common complaints of people seeking emotional counseling is that they feel rejected. They feel that nobody really likes them, that nobody cares for them, or that everybody is highly critical of them. Often they will feel that this is doubly unfair because basically they like everybody. They feel that they pretty much lack any rejecting tendencies themselves. They bend over backwards to be friendly and uncritical of others. But these are exactly the two distinguishing marks of projection: you lack the trait, everybody else has lots of it. But, as every child knows, "It takes one to know one." The person who feels everybody is rejecting him is really one who is totally unaware of his own tendencies to reject and criticize others. These tendencies could be a minor aspect of his total personality, but if he is unaware of them, he will project them on *everybody* he sees and knows. This multiplies the original impulse, and so the world begins to look ominously critical of him in proportions that simply are not there.

The point, true of all projections, is that some people may indeed be very critical of you. But this won't overwhelm you unless you add to their real criticism your own *projected* criticism. Thus, any time you feel intense feelings of inferiority and rejection, it would be wise to look *first* for a projection, and admit that you can be a little bit more critical of the world than you know.

It should be apparent by now that shadow projection not only distorts our view of reality "out there," it also greatly changes our feeling of self "in here." When I project some emotion or trait as shadow, I still continue to perceive it but only in a distorted and illusory fashion—it appears as an "object out there." Likewise, I still continue to *feel* the shadow, but only in a distorted and disguised fashion—once the shadow is projected, I *feel* it only as a *symptom*.

Thus, as we have just seen, if I project my own hostility toward people, I will imagine that people are harboring hostile feelings for me, and thus I will begin to feel a creeping fear of people in general. My original hostility has become my projected shadow. So I "see" it only in other people and I feel it in myself only as the symptom of fear. My shadow has become my symptom.

So when I try to cast out my shadow, I do not become free of it. I am not left with a vacancy, a gap, or a blank space in my personality. I am left with a symptom, a painful reminder that I'm unaware of some facet of myself. Further, once my shadow has become my symptom, I will then *fight my symptom as I once fought my shadow*. When I try to deny any of my own tendencies (shadow), these tendencies show up as symptoms, and I then dislike the symptoms with the same force I once disliked the shadow. I will probably even try to hide my symptoms (of trembling, inferiority, depression, anxiety, etc.) from other people, just as I once tried to hide my shadow from myself.

So each symptom—a depression, anxiety, boredom, or fear—contains some facet of the shadow, some projected emotion or trait or character-istic. It is important to understand that our symptoms, as uncomfortable as they may be, must not be resisted, despised, or avoided, because they contain the key to their own dissolution. To fight a symptom is merely to fight the shadow contained in the symptom, and this is precisely what caused the problem in the first place.

As the first step in therapy on this level, we need to make room for our symptoms, give them space, actually start to befriend the uncomfortable feelings, called symptoms, that we have heretofore despised. We must touch our symptoms with awareness and as much open acceptance as we can command. And this means to *allow* oneself to feel depressed, anxious, rejected, bored, hurt, or embarrassed. It means that where for-merly we resisted these feelings in all sorts of ways, we now simply allow these feelings to display themselves. Indeed, we actively encourage them. We invite the symptom right into our home, and we let it move and breathe freely, while we simply try to remain aware of it in its own form. That, very simply, is the first step in therapy, and in many cases it is all that is required, for the moment we truly accept a symptom we also accept a large part of the shadow concealed in that symptom. The prob-lem then tends to disappear.

If the symptom is persistent, we proceed to the second step of therapy on the persona level. The instructions for the second step are simple, but its execution demands time and perseverance. All we do is begin to consciously *translate* any symptom back to its original form. For this translation, you might use as a dictionary the broad guidelines set forth in this chapter (see table) and in the recommended readings. The essence of this second step is to realize that any symptom is simply a *signal* (or symbol) of some unconscious shadow tendency. Thus, for example, you might feel that you are under some very strong pressures at work. Now, as we have seen, the *symptom* of pressure is always an indication, a simple *signal*, that you have more drive for the job than you know or are willing to admit. You might wish not to openly admit your real interest and desire so that you can extort guilt from others for all the thankless hours of work you "have" to perform for "their" benefit. Or you might wish to parlay your "selfless" devotion into a bigger payoff. Or you might have innocently lost track of your drive. Whatever the reason, the symptom of pressure is a sure sign that you are more eager than you know. Thus, you can translate the symptom back to its original and correct form. "I have to" becomes "I want to."

Translation is the key to therapy. For instance, in order to dispel pres-

THE COMMON MEANING OF VARIOUS SHADOW SYMPTOMS
*A Dictionary for Translating Symptoms
Back to Their Original Shadow Forms*

Symptom TRANSLATED TO	*Its Original Shadow Form*
Pressure	Drive
Rejection ("Nobody likes me.")	"I wouldn't give them the time of day!"
Guilt ("You make me feel guilty.")	"I resent your demands."
Anxiety	Excitement
Self-consciousness ("Everybody's looking at me.")	"I'm more interested in people than I know."
Impotence/frigidity	"I wouldn't give him/her the satisfaction."
Fear ("They want to hurt me.")	Hostility ("I'm angry and attacking without knowing it.")
Sad	Mad!
Withdrawn	"I'll push you all away!"
I can't.	"I won't, damnit!"
Obligation ("I have to.")	Desire ("I want to.")
Hatred ("I despise you for X.")	Autobiographical gossip ("I dislike X in myself.")
Envy (You're sooo great.")	"I'm a bit better than I know."

sure, you do not have to *invent* drive, or try to feel drive that isn't there, or conjure up drive you now seem to lack. I am not saying that if you can force yourself to feel drive and interest in a job, that you will then feel no pressure. I am saying that *if* you feel pressure, the necessary drive *is already present* but is disguised as the symptom of pressure. You do not have to conjure up drive and place it next to the feelings of pressure. Those feelings of pressure are already the drive you need. You simply have to call those feelings of pressure by their original and correct name: *drive*. It's a simple translation, not a creation.

So, in just this way, symptoms—far from being undesirable—are opportunities for growth. Symptoms point very accurately to your unconscious shadow; they are infallible signals of some projected tendency. Through your symptoms you find your shadow, and through your shadow you find growth, and expansion of boundaries, a path to an accurate and acceptable self-image. You have, in short, descended from persona level to ego level. It's almost as simple as this: persona + shadow = ego.

It would be remiss of me to close this chapter without offering a simple key for understanding the essence of the therapeutic work to be done on this level. If you disregard the technical jargon of any shadow therapist, and just listen to the overall drift of his conversation, you will find that what he says follows a certain pattern. If you say you love your mother, he will say you unconsciously hate her. If you say you hate her, he will say you unconsciously love her. If you say you can't stand being depressed, he will say you actually court it. If you say you hate being humiliated, he will say you secretly love it. If you are passionately involved in a religious, political, or ideological crusade to convert others to your beliefs, he will suggest that you don't really believe in them at all, that your crusading is merely an attempt to convert your own disbelieving self. If you say yes, he says no. If you say up, he says down. If you say meow, he says bark. And then if you say that you always suspected that you hated psychologists and now you're sure, he'll say you're really a frustrated psychologist and that you secretly envy all therapists.

This starts to sound silly, but under all the apparently convoluted logic, therapists, whether they realize it or not, are simply *confronting you with your own opposites*. We can look at all the examples in this chapter from this angle, and the fact is, in each of these situations, the individual was aware of only one side of the opposites. The individual refused to see *both* opposites, to realize the unity of these polarities. Since the opposites cannot exist without each other, if you aren't aware of both of them, you will send the rejected pole underground. You will render it unconscious, and thus project it. You will, in short, create a boundary between the opposites, and thus generate a battle. But this is a battle that can never be won, only perpetually lost in way after painful way, because the two sides are actually aspects of each other.

The shadow, then, is simply your unconscious opposites. Thus, a simple way to contact your shadow is to assume the very opposite of whatever you now consciously intend, wish, or desire. That will show you exactly how your shadow looks at the world, and it is this view which you will want to befriend. This does not mean to *act* on your opposites, merely to be aware of them. If you feel you intensely dislike someone, be aware of the side of you that likes the person. If you are madly in love, be aware of the part of you that couldn't care less. If you hate a particular feeling or symptom, be aware of that aspect of yourself which secretly enjoys it. The moment you are truly aware of your opposites, of both the positive and negative feelings toward any situation, then many tensions connected with that situation drop out, because the battle of opposites which created that tension is dissolved. On the other hand, the moment you lose the unity of opposites, the awareness of both sides in yourself, then you split the opposites apart, erect a boundary between them, and thus render the rejected pole unconscious where it returns to plague you as symptom. Since the opposites are always a unity, the only way they can be separated is by unconsciousness—selective inattention.

As you begin to explore your opposites, your shadow, your projections, you will begin to find that you are assuming responsibility for your own feelings and your own states of mind. You will start to see that most battles between you and other people are really battles between you and your projected opposites. You will start to see that your symptoms are not something that the environment is doing to you, but something you are doing to yourself as an exaggerated substitute for what you would really like to do to others. You will find that people and events don't cause you to be upset, but are merely the occasions for you to upset yourself. It is a tremendous relief when you first understand that you yourself are producing your own symptoms, because that also means you can *stop* producing those symptoms by translating them back to their original form. You become the cause of your own feelings, and not the effect.

What we have seen in this chapter is how, by trying to deny certain facets of our ego, we wind up with a false and distorted self-image, called the persona. In general, a boundary is erected between what you like (persona) and what you don't (shadow). We also saw that these denied facets of our ego (the shadow) end up projected so as to appear to exist "out there" in the environment. We then are left shadow-boxing our way through life. The boundary between persona and shadow becomes a battle between persona and shadow, and the war within is felt as a symptom. We then hate our symptoms with the same passion with which we originally hated our shadow; and with the shadow projected onto other people, we hate these people as we once hated the shadow. We then treat others as a symptom: something to be fought. And so the manifold forms of battle proceed across this level's boundary.

To develop a more or less accurate self-image—that is, to descend from persona to ego—is simply to gain a comprehensive awareness of those facets of yourself which you didn't know existed. And these facets

are easily spotted because they show up as your symptoms, your opposites, your projections. To take back your projections is simply to tear
down a boundary, to include as yourself things which you thought were
foreign; to make room in yourself for an understanding and acceptance
of all your various potentials, negative and positive, good and bad, lov-
able and despicable, and thus to develop a relatively accurate image of
everything your psychophysical organism is. It is to shift your boundaries, to remap your soul so that old enemies are allies and secretly fighting opposites become open friends. In the end, while you will not find
all of you desirable, you might find all of you likeable.

RECOMMENDATIONS

Although psychoanalysis remains the classic approach to the ego level
(i.e., to helping an individual living as persona descend to the ego level),
I can no longer recommend this procedure as the therapy of choice, even
if you can afford the money and the time. First, there are quicker methods that are at least as effective. Second, analysis itself so often twists
the insights that spontaneously arise from the deeper levels of the spectrum that it tends to reduce the depths of the soul to bland uniformity.
The theory of psychoanalysis, however, remains essential to an understanding of the dynamics of the ego, persona, and shadow, and a good
introduction is Calvin Hall, *A Primer of Freudian Psychology* (New
York: Mentor, 1973). The advanced student might try Freud's own *A
General Introduction to Psychoanalysis* (New York: Pocket, 1971). Serious readers are directed to Otto Fenichel, *The Psychoanalytic Theory of
Neurosis* (New York: Norton, 1972).

Books dealing with more recent approaches to the persona/ego include William Glasser, *Reality Therapy* (New York: Harper, 1965); A.
Ellis and R. Harper, *A New Guide to Rational Living* (Hollywood: Wilshire Books, 1975); M. Maltz, *Psychocybernetics* (Hollywood: Wilshire
Books, 1960); Karen Horney, *Self-Analysis* (New York: Norton, 1942;
Horney had some decidedly centauric/holistic trends in her approach,
which makes her works useful on both ego and centaur levels). M.
Werthman, *Self-Psyching* (Los Angeles: Tarcher, 1978), is a nice com-
pendium of techniques, most of which aim at egoic problems. Putney
and Putney, *The Adjusted American* (New York: Harper, 1966), is a
marvelous book; I have drawn many of the examples in this chapter
from their volume, a debt I gratefully acknowledge. Gestalt therapy also

deals with the shadow very effectively, but since it also works with the centaur level, I have included the relevant material in that chapter.

The approach of choice seems to be, at least to my mind, Transactional Analysis. It preserves the essentials of Freud, but sets them in a context that is simple, clear, concise. Further, it generally recognizes the possibility of deeper levels of one's being, and thus does not overtly sabotage deeper insights. See T. Harris, *I'm OK—You're OK* (New York: Avon, 1969); and Eric Berne's *Games People Play* (New York: Grove, 1967) and *What Do You Say After You Say Hello?* (New York: Bantam, 1974).

8

The Centaur Level

WE SAW IN THE LAST chapter that by touching and eventually re-owning our projected shadow, we could "expand" our identity from an impoverished persona to a healthy ego. We could heal the split, dissolve the boundary, between persona and shadow, and thus find a larger and more stable sense of self-identity. It's almost like moving from a cramped apartment into a comfortable home. In this chapter we go on from the comfortable home to a spacious mansion. We continue the basic process of boundary dissolution, but to a deeper level, exploring some of the methods to expand identity from the ego (and its world view) to the centaur by touching and re-owning our projected bodies.

To re-own the body might initially strike one as a peculiar notion. The boundary between ego and flesh is so deeply embedded in the average person's unconscious that he responds to the proposed task of healing this split with a curious mixture of puzzlement and boredom. He has come to believe that the boundary between the mind and body is unalterably real, and thus he can't figure out why anyone would want to tamper with it, let alone dissolve it.

As it turns out, few of us have lost our minds, but most of us have long ago lost our bodies, and I'm afraid we must take that literally. It seems, in fact, that "I" am almost sitting on my body as if I were a horseman riding on a horse. I beat it or praise it, I feed and clean and nurse it when necessary. I urge it on without consulting it and I hold it back against its will. When my body-horse is well-behaved I generally ignore it, but when it gets unruly—which is all too often—I pull out the whip to beat it back into reasonable submission.

Indeed, my body seems to just dangle along under me. I no longer approach the world *with* my body but *on* my body. I'm up here, it's down there, and I'm basically uneasy about just what it is that *is* down there. My consciousness is almost *exclusively* head consciousness—I *am* my head, but I *own* my body. The body is reduced from self to property, something which is "mine" but not "me." The body, in short, becomes an object or a projection, in just the same way the shadow did. A boundary is erected upon the total organism so that the body is projected as not-self. This boundary is a split, a fissure, or, in the words of Lowen, a *block:* "The block also operates to separate and isolate the psychic realm from the somatic realm. Our consciousness tells us that each acts upon the other, but because of the block it does not extend deep enough for us to sense the underlying unity. In effect the block creates a split in the unity of the personality. Not only does it dissociate the psyche from the soma, but it also separates surface phenomena from their roots in the depths of the organism."

What fundamentally concerns us here is the *disruption of the total organism,* the centaur, of which the loss of the body is only the most visible and sensible sign. The loss of the body is not precisely synonymous with the disruption of the centaur, "the underlying unity," but is merely one of the manifestations that this disruption make take. Nevertheless, it is the one to which we will confine our attention in this chapter, inasmuch as it is the easiest to grasp and the simplest to communicate. Please remember, however, that I am not saying that the body per se—what we call the "physical body"—is a deeper reality than the mental-ego. In fact, the simple body itself is the lowest of all modes of consciousness, so simple that we have not even included it, by itself, in this book. The body is not a "deeper reality" than the ego, as many somatologists think, but the *integration* of the body *and* the ego is indeed a deeper reality than either alone, and that integration is what we will emphasize in this chapter, even if, for practical purposes, we dwell on the physical body and physical body exercises.

There are, as one would expect, all sorts of reasons why we abandon our bodies, and why we now fear to reclaim them, some of which we have already outlined in the discussion of the evolution of the spectrum. On a superficial level, we refuse to reclaim the body because we just don't think there's any reason to—it seems a big to-do about nothing. On a deeper level, we fear to reclaim the body because it houses, in a particularly vivid and living form, strong emotions and feelings which are socially taboo. And ultimately, the body is avoided because it is the abode of death.

For all these reasons, and more, a generally "adjusted" person has long ago projected her body as an "object out there," or, we might say, as an object "down there." The centaur is abandoned, and the person identifies with the ego as against the body. But, like all projections, this alienation of the body only results in the projected body returning to haunt the individual, clobbering her in the most agonizing of ways, and worse yet, with her own energy. Since the body is for all purposes placed on the *other* side of the self/not-self boundary, since it is not befriended, since it is no longer an ally, it naturally becomes an enemy. The ego and the body square off, and an intense if sometimes subtle war of opposites begins.

Since, as we have seen, every boundary creates two warring opposites, the same is naturally true for the boundary between the ego and the body. There are a number of important opposites which come to be associated with this particular boundary, but one of the most significant is that of the *voluntary* vs. the *involuntary*. The ego is the seat of control, of manipulation, of voluntary and willed activity. In fact, the ego as a rule identifies itself only with voluntary processes. Yet the body is basically a well-organized collection of involuntary processes, of circulation, digestion, growth and differentiation, metabolism, and so on. If this sounds odd, just notice the speech of the average person, and listen carefully to those processes she calls herself. She will say, "*I* move my arm," but she will *not* say, "I beat my heart." She will say, "*I* am eating my food," but she will *not* say, "I am digesting my food." She will say, "I close my eyes," but she will not say, "I grow my hair." She will say, "I wiggle my toes," but she will not say, "I circulate my blood."

In other words, she, as ego, will identify only with those actions which are voluntary and controllable; and *all the rest,* all the spontaneous and involuntary actions, she feels are somehow not-self and untrustable. Despite the common sense notions to the contrary, doesn't it seem odd that you identify with only a fraction of your total being? Isn't it strange that you call at best one-half of the organism "you"? To whom does the other half belong?

In a sense, the ego feels trapped, a victim of the unruly capriciousness of its own body. It is thus not unusual to find those who feel enchained by the flesh, and long for a state of affairs, now or after death, where the soul rules supreme, unencumbered by the tender vulnerability of flesh, disembodied and floating in air, covered by nothing more substantial than a white satin nightie. It's easy to see why in the eyes of many, flesh and sin are so terribly synonymous.

The ego feels especially trapped by the body's vulnerability to pain. Pain, suffering, the intense sensitivity of living tissue and raw nerves—these understandably enough terrorize the ego, and it seeks to withdraw from the source of pain, to numb and freeze the body so as to reduce its vulnerability to painful vibrations. Although the ego cannot control the body's involuntary sensations, it can and does learn to withdraw awareness from the body, to globally deaden and desensitize it. This is what Aurobindo called "vital shock"—the shock and recoil of awareness from the vulnerability and mortality of the flesh, a recoil that numbs the flesh and distorts awareness.

But this body-deadening is accomplished only at a heavy price. For if it is true that the body is the source of pain, it is also true that it is the source of pleasure. The ego, in killing the source of pain, at the same time kills the source of pleasure. No more suffering . . . and no more joy.

Thus the normal person freezes the body without comprehending the nature of this freeze-out. He does not even know that he is frozen. It's almost like a pervasive case of frostbite. The victim of frostbite doesn't realize he has it, because the affected area lacks all feeling and he can't feel the lack of feeling. He feels nothing, which seems just fine.

This pervasive lack of feeling is the general result of vital shock, of our recoil from the body and our disruption of the centaur. This disruption accompanies, to one degree or another, even the healthy ego. For as long as you are identified exclusively with the ego, then by definition your self does not include or integrate the spontaneous processes of the organism. Thus, even though we may have expanded from persona to ego, we may realize that we somehow lack a sense of depth, a ground of *meaningful* feeling, a wellspring of inner awareness and feeling-attention. Hence, we might be moved to continue the process of descent, to let go of our narrowed identity with just the ego and discover the felt identity with the total psychophysical organism. To the therapists who work on this level, this means the discovery of an authentic, existential self.

We will be exploring ways to dissolve the boundary between the mind and body so as to discover again this unity of opposites lying asleep in the depths of our being. "This split cannot be overcome," says Lowen, "by a knowledge of the energetic processes in the body. Knowledge itself is a surface phenomenon and belongs to the realm of the ego. One has to feel the flow and sense the course of the excitation in the body. To do this, however, one must give up the rigidity of one's ego control so that the deep body sensations can reach the surface."

Simple as it sounds, that is the very difficulty almost every person faces as he tries to connect with his body. He won't really feel his legs, stomach, or shoulders, but, out of habit, he thinks about his legs, stomach, and shoulders. He pictures them to himself and thus avoids giving feeling-attention to them directly. This is, of course, one of the very mechanisms responsible for the dissociation of the body in the first place. Special attention should be given this tendency to conceptualize our feelings, and a special effort made to suspend, at least temporarily, this habitual translation of feeling-attention into thoughts and pictures.

One way to begin connecting with the body is by lying down on your back, outstretched, on a rug or mat. Simply close your eyes, breathe deeply but easily, and begin to explore your bodily feelings. Don't *try* to feel anything, don't force feelings, just let your attention flow through your body and note if any feeling, positive or negative, is present in the various parts of the body. Can you, for example, feel your legs? your stomach? your heart? eyes? genitals, buttocks, scalp, diaphragm, feet? Notice which parts of the body seem alive with feeling, full and strong and vital, and which parts seem dull, heavy, lifeless, dimmed, tight, or painful. Try this for at least three minutes, and notice how often your attention might leave the body and wander into daydreams. Does it strike you as odd that it might be very difficult to stay in your body for three minutes? If you're not in the body, where are you?

After this preliminary, we can move to the next step: still lying with your arms alongside and legs slightly parted, eyes closed, breathe very deeply but slowly, *drawing the inhalation from the throat to the abdomen,* eventually filling up your entire midsection. Imagine, if you like, that your entire chest and stomach are lined with a large balloon and that with each inhalation you are totally filling the balloon. The "balloon" should softly extend into the chest and bulge out fully and strongly in the abdomen. If you can't feel the gentle force of the expanded balloon in any of these areas, simply let the balloon fill out a little more, extending itself into that particular area. Then exhale slowly and smoothly, allowing the balloon to empty completely. Repeat this seven or eight times, maintaining the gentle but firm pressure inside the balloon so it bulges the abdomen and reaches the pelvic basin. Note especially which areas feel tight, tense, painful, or numb.

Can you feel that the entire ballooned area is one piece, or does it seem divided and segmented into chest, abdomen, and pelvic floor, each segment separated from the others by areas or bands of tightness, tension, or pain? In spite of these minor pains and discomforts, you might begin to notice that the feeling which extends throughout the balloon is one of subtle pleasure and joy. You are literally breathing in pleasure and radiating it throughout your bodymind. Upon exhalation, do not lose or exhaust the breath, but release it as pleasure to permeate the entire body. In this way, subtle pleasure flows through your bodymind and becomes fuller with each cycle. If you are not sure of this, complete another three or four total expansion breaths, yielding to the pleasure involved.

Perhaps you can start to understand why yogis call the breath a *vital force*—not in the philosophical sense, but in the feeling sense. Upon inhalation, you draw in a vital force from the throat to the abdomen, charging the body with energy and life. Upon exhalation, you release and radiate this force as subtle pleasure and joy throughout the bodymind itself.

You might continue the total expansion balloon breathing, inhaling vital force *from* the throat *to* the navel-abdomen (the "hara"), but start to feel the exhalation as a vital force radiating outward from the abdomen to all parts of the body. With each inhalation from the throat, charge the hara with vitality. Then, upon exhalation, see how far down and into each leg you can feel (or follow) the vital force or pleasure radiate—into the thighs? knees? feet? It eventually should go literally to the tips of the toes. Continue this for several breaths, and then try the same thing with the upper extremities. Can you feel the vitality being released into your arms? fingers? head, brain, and scalp? Then, upon exhalation, allow this subtle pleasure to pass through your body and *into the world at large*. Release your breath, through the body, to infinity.

Putting all these components together, we arrive at a complete breathing cycle: Upon inhalation, draw the breath *from* the throat *to* the hara, charging it with vital force. Upon exhalation, release this subtle pleasure *through* the entire bodymind *to* the world, to the cosmos, to infinity. Once this cycle becomes full, then start to allow all thinking to dissolve in the exhalation and pass to infinity. Do the same with all distressful feelings, with disease, with suffering, with pain. Allow feeling-attention to pass through all present conditions and then beyond them to infinity, moment to moment to moment.

We come now to the specifics of this type of exercise. More than likely you were able to feel vital pleasure and feeling-attention circulate easily throughout your bodymind. But in each aspect of this exercise you might also have felt some area of numbness, lack of feeling, or deadness on the one hand, or tightness, tension, rigidity, or pain on the other. You felt, in other words, blocks (mini-boundaries) to the full flow of feeling-attention. Most people invariably feel tightness and tension in the neck, eyes, anus, diaphragm, shoulders, or lower back. Numbness is often found in the pelvic area, genitals, heart, lower abdomen, or the extremities. It's important to discover, as best you can, just where your own particular blocks exist. For the moment, *don't try to get rid of them.* At best, that won't work and at worst it will tighten them. Just find out where they seem to be, and mentally note the locations.

Once you have pinpointed these blocks, you can begin the process of dissolving them. But first we might consider just what these blocks and resistances mean—these areas of bands of tightness, pressure, and tension anchored throughout the body. We saw that on the ego level a person could resist and avoid an impulse or emotion by denying ownership of it. Through the mechanism of egoic projection, a person could prevent the awareness of a particular shadow tendency in himself. If he actually felt very hostile, but denied his own hostility, he would project it and thus feel that the world was attacking him. In other words, he would feel anxiety and fear, the result of projected hostility.

What is happening in the body when this hostility is projected? Mentally, a projection has occurred, but physically something else must happen simultaneously, since mind and body are not two. What happens in the body when you repress hostility? How, on the body level, do you suppress a strong emotion which seeks discharge in some activity?

If you get very hostile and angry, you might discharge this emotion in the activities of screaming, yelling, and striking out with the arms and fists. These muscular activities are the very essence of hostility itself. Thus, if you are to suppress hostility, you can only do so by physically suppressing these *muscular* discharge activities. You must, in other words, use your muscles to hold back these discharge activities. Rather, you must use *some* of your muscles to hold back the action of *some* of your other muscles. What results is a war of muscles. Half of your muscles struggle to discharge the hostility by striking out, while the other half strain to prevent just that. It's like stepping on the gas with one foot and the brake with the other. The conflict ends in stalemate, but a very tense one, with large amounts of energy expended with a net movement of zero.

In the case of suppressing hostility, you will probably clamp the muscles of your jaw, throat, neck, shoulders, and upper arms, for this is the only way you can physically "hold in" hostility. And hostility denied, as we have seen, usually floats into your awareness as fear. Thus, the next time you are in the grip of an irrational fear, notice that your whole shoulder area is pulled in and up, the sign that you are holding in hostility, and therefore feeling fear. But in your shoulders themselves you will *no longer feel* the tendency to reach out and attack; you will no longer feel hostility; you will only feel a strong tension, tightness, pressure. You have a block.

This is precisely the nature of the blocks which you located throughout your body during the breathing exercises. Every block, every tension or pressure in the body, is basically a *muscular* holding-in of some taboo impulse or feeling. That these blocks are muscular is an extremely important point, a point to which we will return very shortly. For now, we need only note that these blocks and bands of tension are the result of two sets of muscles fighting each other (across a mini-boundary), one set seeking to discharge the impulse, one set seeking to hold it in. And this is an active holding in, an "in-holding" or in-hibiting. You literally crush yourself in certain areas instead of letting-out the impulse associated with that area.

Thus, if you find a tension around the eyes, you might be in-holding a desire to cry. If you find a tension-ache in your temples, you may be clamping your jaws together unknowingly, perhaps trying to prevent screaming, yelling, or even laughing. A tension in the shoulder and neck indicates suppressed or in-held anger, rage, or hostility, while a tension in the diaphragm indicates that you chronically restrict and in-hold your breathing in an attempt to control the display of wayward emotions or feeling-attention in general. (During any act of self-control, most people will hold their breath.) Tension through the lower abdomen and pelvic floor usually means you have cut off all awareness of your sexuality, that you stiffen-up and in-hold that area to prevent the vital force of breath and energy from flowing through. Should this occur—for whatever reason—you will also shut off most feeling in your legs. And a tension, rigidity, or lack of strength in your legs usually indicates lack of rootedness, stability, groundedness, or balance in general.

Thus, as we have just seen, one of the best ways to understand the general *meaning* of a particular block is by noting where it occurs in the body. Particular body areas usually discharge particular emotions. You probably don't scream with your feet, cry with your knees, or have orgasms in your elbows. So if there is a block in a particular body area, we can assume the corresponding emotion is being suppressed and in-held. In this regard, the works of Lowen and Keleman (listed at the end of this chapter) are excellent guides.

Assuming you have now more or less located your major blocks to feeling, you can proceed to the really interesting endeavor: releasing and dissolving the blocks themselves. Although the basic procedure is simple to comprehend and easy enough to perform, the fruition of conscious results takes much hard work, effort, and patience. You probably have spent at least 15 years building up a specific block, so you shouldn't be surprised if it doesn't vanish permanently after 15 minutes of work. Like all boundaries, these take time to dissolve in conscious awareness.

If you have encountered these blocks before, you will realize that the most annoying aspect of them is that no matter how hard you try, you can't seem to relax them, at least not permanently. Through conscious effort you might succeed in going limp for a few minutes, but the tension (in your neck, back, chest, etc.) returns with a vengeance the moment you forget this "forced relaxation." Some blocks and tensions—perhaps most—refuse to relax at all. And yet the only remedy we habitually apply is the futile attempt to consciously relax these tensions (an approach, paradoxically enough, which itself demands a rather exhausting effort).

It seems, in other words, that these blocks happen to us, that they occur against our will, that they are wholly involuntary and uninvited. We seem to be their uncomfortable victims. Let us see, then, just what is involved in the persistence of these uninvited guests.

The first thing to notice is that these blocks are all muscular, as we mentioned earlier. Each block is actually a contraction, a tightening, a locking of some muscle or group of muscles. Some group of *skeletal* muscles, that is, and *every skeletal muscle is under voluntary control.* The same voluntary muscles you use to move an arm, to chew, to walk, to jump, to make a fist, or to kick—just these same muscles are operating in every body block.

But that means that these blocks are not—indeed, they physically *cannot*—be involuntary. They do not happen to us. They are and must be something we are actively doing to ourselves. In short, we have deliberately, intentionally, and voluntarily created these blocks, since they consist solely of voluntary muscles.

Yet, curiously enough, we *don't know* that we are creating them. We are tightening these muscles, and although we know that they are tight and tense, we do not know that *we* are actively tensing them. Once this type of block occurs, we can't relax these muscles, simply because we don't know we are contracting them in the first place. It then appears that these blocks happen all by themselves (just like all other unconscious processes), and we seem helpless victims crushed by forces "beyond" our control.

This whole situation is almost exactly as if I were pinching myself but didn't know it. It is as if I intentionally pinched myself, but then forgot it was I who was doing the pinching. I feel the pain of the pinching, but cannot figure out why it won't stop. Just so, all of these muscular tensions anchored in my body are deep-seated forms of self-pinching. So the important question is *not*, "How can I stop or relax these blocks?" but rather, "How can I see that *I* am actively producing them?" If you are pinching yourself but don't know it, to ask somebody else to stop the pain does no good. To ask how to stop pinching yourself implies that *you aren't* doing it yourself. On the other hand, as soon as you see that you are actively pinching yourself, then, and only then, do you spontaneously stop. You don't go around asking how to stop pinching yourself, any more than you ask how to raise your hand. They are both voluntary actions.

The crux, therefore, is getting the direct feel of how I actively tense these muscles, and therefore the one thing I *don't* do is try to relax them. Rather, I must, as always, play my opposites. I must do what I would have never thought of doing before: I must actively and consciously attempt to *increase* the particular tension. By deliberately increasing the tension, I am making my self-pinching activity conscious instead of unconscious. In short, I start to remember how *I* have been pinching myself. I see how I have literally been attacking myself. That understanding felt through-and-through releases energy from the war of muscles, energy which I can then direct outward toward the environment instead of inward on myself. Instead of squeezing and attacking myself, I can "attack" a job, a book, a good meal, and thus learn afresh the correct meaning of the word aggression: "to move toward."

But there is a second and equally important aspect of dissolving these blocks. We have just seen that the first is to deliberately increase the pressure or tension by further tightening the muscles involved. In this way we do consciously what we have heretofore been doing unconsciously. But remember that these tension blocks were serving a most significant function—they were initially introduced to choke off feelings and impulses that at one time seemed dangerous, taboo, or unacceptable. These blocks were, and still are, forms of *resistance* to particular emotions. Thus, if these blocks are to be permanently dissolved, you will have to open yourself to the emotions which lie buried beneath the muscular cramp.

It should be emphasized that these "buried feelings" are not some sort of wildly insatiable and totally overpowering orgiastic demands, nor some form of demonically possessing and bestial urges to wipe out your father and mother and siblings. They are most often rather mild, although they might seem dramatic because you have muscularly in-held them so long. They usually involve a release of tears, a good scream or two, ability for uninhibited orgasm, a good old-fashioned temper tantrum, or a temporary but enraged attack upon pillows set up for that purpose. Even if some fairly strong negative emotion surges up—some full-blown rage—it need not cause great alarm, for it does not constitute a major portion of your personality. In a live theatre play, when a minor two-line character walks on stage for the first time, all eyes in the audience turn to this minor player, even though he is an insignificant part of the total cast. Likewise, when some negative emotion first walks into the stage of your awareness, you might become temporarily transfixed with it, even though it too is but a fragment of the total cast of your emotions. Much better to have it up front than rambling around back stage.

In any case, this emotional release, this upsurge of some type of in-held emotion, will usually happen of itself as you begin to consciously take responsibility for increasing the tightening of the muscles in the various blocks of the body. As you deliberately begin to contract the muscles involved, you tend to remember what it is you are contracting your muscles against. For example, if you see a friend about to cry, and you say, "Whatever you do, fight it!" she will probably burst into tears. At that moment she is deliberately trying to in-hold something natural to the organism, and she knows that she is trying to block it, so the emotion cannot easily go underground. In the same way, as you deliberately take charge of your blocks while trying to increase them, the inhibited emotion may start to surface and exhibit itself.

The entire procedure for this type of body awareness experiment might run as follows: After locating a specific block—let's say a tenseness in the jaw, throat, and temples—you give it your full awareness, feeling out just where the tension is and what muscles seem to be involved. Then, slowly but deliberately begin to increase that tension and pressure; in this case, by tightening your throat muscles and clamping your teeth together. While you are experimenting with increasing the muscular pressure, remind yourself that you are not just clamping muscles, *you are actively trying to hold something in.* You can even repeat to yourself (out loud if your jaws aren't involved), "No! I won't! I'm resisting!" so that you truly feel that part of yourself that *is* doing the pinching, that is trying to in-hold some feeling. Then you can slowly release the muscles—and at the same time open yourself totally to whatever feeling would like to surface. In this case, it might be a desire to cry, or to bite out, or to vomit, or to laugh, or to scream. Or it might only be a pleasurable glow where the block used to be. To allow a genuine release of blocked emotions requires time, effort, openness, and some honest work. If you have a typically persistent block, daily "workouts" of 15 minutes or so for upwards of a month will almost certainly be necessary for significant results. The block is released when feeling-attention can flow through that area in a full and perfectly unobstructed fashion on its way to infinity.

An important change in one's sense of self and reality results from this simple healing of the split between the mind and body, the voluntary and involuntary, the willed and the spontaneous. To the extent you can feel your involuntary body processes as *you,* you can begin to *accept* as perfectly natural all manner of things which you cannot *control.* You may more readily accept the uncontrollable and rest easily in the spontaneous, with faith in a deeper self which goes beyond the superficial will and ego rumblings. You may learn you needn't control yourself in order to accept yourself. In fact your deeper self, your centaur, lies beyond your control. It is voluntary *and* involuntary, both perfectly acceptable as manifestations of *you.*

Further, accepting as yourself both the voluntary and the involuntary means that you no longer feel a victim of your body or of involuntary and spontaneous processes in general. You develop a deep sense of responsibility, not in the sense that you are in conscious control of everything that happens and therefore accountable for it, but in the sense that you no longer need to blame or credit anyone else for how you feel. Ultimately, you *are* the deep source producing all your involuntary and voluntary processes, and not its victim.

To accept the involuntary as yourself does not mean you can control the involuntary. You will not be able to make your hair grow faster or your stomach stop grumbling or your blood flow backwards. Rather, by realizing these processes are *just as much you as the voluntary ones,* you give up that chronic but fruitless program to take charge of creation, to obsessively manipulate and compulsively control yourself and your world. Paradoxically, this realization brings about an expanded sense of freedom. Your willful ego can consciously deal with perhaps two or three things at one time. Yet your total organism, without any help from the ego, is at this moment coordinating literally millions of processes at once, from the intricacies of digestion to the complexities of neurotransmission to the coordination of conceptual information. This requires wisdom infinitely greater than the superficial tricks of which the ego is so proud. The more we are capable of resting in the centaur, the more we are capable of founding our lives on, and giving our lives over to, this wider store of natural wisdom and freedom.

Most of our everyday problems and worries stem from trying to control or manipulate processes which the organism would be handling perfectly if it weren't for the intervention of the ego. For example, the ego misguidedly attempts to manufacture happiness, pleasure, or simple joy in living. We feel that pleasure is something intrinsically lacking in the present situation, and that we must manufacture it by surrounding ourselves with sophisticated toys and gadgets. This reinforces the illusion that happiness and pleasure can be piped in from the outside, an illusion which itself is responsible for blocking pleasure, so that we end up striving for that which prevents our own joy.

To come back to the centaur is to realize that mental and physical well-being already circulate within the total psychophysical organism. "Energy is eternal delight, and is from the body," said Blake, and this is a delight which does not depend upon external rewards or promises. It springs from within, and is freely given in this present moment. Whereas the ego lives in time, with its neck outstretched to future gains and its heart lamenting past losses, the centaur lives always in the *nunc fluens,* the passing and concrete present, the lively present which neither clings to yesterday nor screams for tomorrow, but finds its fulfillment in the bounties of this moment (this is not the eternal present, the *nunc stans,* but it is a step in the right direction). Centauric awareness is a powerful antidote to the world of future shock.

Not only might you learn to accept both the voluntary and the involuntary as yourself, you might even start to understand that, at this deeper level, voluntary and involuntary are *one.* They are both *spontaneous* activities of the centaur. We already know that the involuntary is spontaneous. But even acts of will and purposeful decisions spring up spontaneously. For what is *behind* an act of will? Another act of will? Do I will to will, or does the will *just happen?* If the former, do I then will to will to will? Do decisions spontaneously occur, or do I decide to decide to decide? In fact, somewhere down the line even voluntary purposeful activity runs into the spontaneity of the centaur, a spontaneity that underlies and unites both voluntary and involuntary. From this deep level the self leads, as Coomaraswamy put it, "a perpetual, uncalculated life in the present."

The most important result of any therapy aiming at this level is the subtle but pervasive change in awareness as one begins to resurrect the centaur and discover one's prior identity with it. This potential is not just a summation of egoic potentials and body potentials, but instead a wholeness which greatly exceeds the sum of its parts. In the words of Rollo May, "Neither the ego nor the body nor the unconscious can be 'autonomous,' but can only exist as parts of a totality. And it is in this totality that will and freedom must have their base." The expanded potentials of this "totality" are commonly known as those for *self-actualization* (Goldstein, Maslow), *autonomy* (Fromm, Riesman), or *meaning in life* (May). The centauric level is *the* great level of the human potential movement, of existentialism, of humanistic therapy, all of which take as their basic assumption the integration of mind, body, and emotions into a higher-order unity, a "deeper totality."

This is no place for a dissertation on self-actualization; the following quote of Maslow really says it all. It points out what self-actualization is, and the results of failing to engage it:

> We have, all of us, an impulse toward actualizing more of our potentialities, toward self-actualization, or full humanness or human fulfillment. [This is] a push toward the establishment of the fully evolved and authentic self . . . , an increased stress on the role of integration (or unity, wholeness). Resolving a dichotomy into a higher, more inclusive unity amounts to healing a split in the person and making him more unified. [This is also an impulse] to be the best, the very best you are capable of becoming. If you deliberately plan to be less than you are capable of being, then I warn you that you'll be deeply unhappy for the rest of your life.

As Maslow suggests, self-actualization and meaning are intimately related. For just this reason, centauric/existential therapists are also deeply concerned with fundamental meaning in life. Not egoic meaning, but something beyond that. For once you have developed an accurate and healthy ego, what then? Once you have met your egoic goals, once you have the car and the house and some self-esteem, once you have accumulated material goods and professional recognition—once all of that, what then? When history runs out of meaning for the soul, when material pursuits in the outer world go flat in their appeal, when it dawns on you for certain that death alone awaits you, what then?

To find egoic meaning in life is to *do* something in life, and up to a point that is appropriate. But beyond the ego is beyond that type of meaning—to a meaning that is less of doing and more of being. As e. e. cummings put it, "If you can be, be. If not, cheer up and go on about other peoples' business, doing and undoing unto others 'til you drop."

To find centauric meaning in life—fundamental meaning—is to find that the very processes of life itself generate joy. Meaning is found, not in outward actions or possessions, but in the inner radiant currents of your own being, and in the *release* and *relationship* of these currents to the world, to friends, to humanity at large, and to infinity itself.

To find real meaning in life is also to accept death in life, to befriend the impermanence of all that is, to release the entire bodymind into emptiness with each exhalation. To yield unconditionally to death on each exhalation is to be reborn and regenerated with each inhalation. On the other hand, to recoil from the death and impermanence of each moment is to recoil from the life of each moment, since the two are one and the same.

All in all, the centaur level is the home of 1) self-actualization, 2) meaning, and 3) existential or life-death concerns. And the resolution of all of these requires a whole-bodied full-minded awareness, a current of feeling-attention which floods the bodymind and utilizes the entire psychophysical being. To identify with the ego *and* the body is actually to change both by setting each in a new context. The ego can reach down to earth—its ground and support—and the body can reach up to heaven—its light and space. The boundary, and the battle, between the two has dissolved, a new set of opposites re-united, and a deeper unity discovered. For the first time, you can embody your mind and mind your body.

RECOMMENDATIONS

There are numerous excellent books dealing with various aspects of the centaur/existential level. Especially recommended are Rollo May, *Love and Will* (New York: Norton, 1969); Carl Rogers, *On Becoming a Per-*

son (Boston: Houghton Mifflin, 1961); Ernest Becker, *The Denial of Death* (New York: Free Press, 1973).

As for approaches to the centaur level, there are three or four that stand out. Hatha yoga, the centuries-tested method, is simple, effective, and easy to perform on one's own. See Swami Vishnudevananda, *Complete Illustrated Book of Yoga* (New York: Pocket, 1972). See also Bubba Free John, *Conscious Exercise and the Transcendental Sun* (San Francisco: Dawn Horse, 1977).

Gestalt therapy embodies an excellent and theoretically sound approach, for which see Perls, Goodman, and Hefferline, *Gestalt Therapy* (New York: Delta, 1951); Fritz Perls, *Gestalt Therapy Verbatim* (Lafayette: Real People Press, 1969). The former is especially recommended, since—besides being the classic theoretical statement of Gestalt therapy—it is designed as a do-it-yourself workbook.

E. T. Gendlin's *Focusing* (New York: Everest House, 1979) is an important statement of the influential school of experiential therapy, which works with the "ongoing psychophysiological flow." Maslow's works are very significant, but since he eventually moved to a transpersonal orientation, his works are listed in that chapter.

Combining elements of noetic analysis with powerful body exercise is Bioenergetic Analysis, an excellent approach to the centaur. It should be at least mentioned, however, that some "practitioners" of bioenergetics regress into a mere glorification of, and obsession with, the simple physical body and bodily exercises, shunning mental-egoic insight and verbalization. These so-called therapies should be avoided—unless they are used in conscious coordination with, or as preliminaries to, egoic or true centauric therapy. Alexander Lowen often seems to strike a happy balance between mental and physical; see *The Betrayal of the Body* (New York: Macmillan, 1967); *Depression and the Body* (Baltimore: Penguin, 1973). See also Stanley Keleman, *Your Body Speaks Its Mind* (New York: Simon and Schuster, 1975).

9

The Self in Transcendence

A S WE NOW LEAVE the centaur level and move toward the transpersonal bands, we leave behind familiarity and common sense orientations to ourselves and our worlds. For we are entering the world of beyond and above, where we begin to touch an awareness that transcends the individual and discloses to a person something which passes far beyond himself. Any sort of legitimate discipline on this level sooner or later opens the individual to an awareness in himself that is so deep and profound that it may lift him out of himself into the vast and subtle world of the transpersonal.

But, alas, such talk as this engenders little more than bewilderment in most modern, well-educated Westerners, for with the general anemia of present-day religion, we have largely lost any direct and socially accessible means to transcendence. The average person will therefore probably listen in disbelief if it is pointed out that she has, nestled in the deepest recesses of her being, a transpersonal self, a self that transcends her individuality and connects her to a world beyond conventional space and time.

It is unfortunate that we in the West, over the past few centuries, have increasingly tended to repress the transcendent. This repression, extensive as it is subtle, is undoubtedly more responsible for the discontents of our present unhappy civilization than any amount of repression of sexuality, hostility, aggression, or other superficial repressions operating on the upper levels of the spectrum. Repressions on the persona, ego, or centaur levels, frantic and dramatic as they may be, are not encompassing enough to set the tone of a whole society, the roots of which are always, knowingly or unknowingly, set in the soil of transcendence. This fact we have somehow managed to collectively deny. However, because the repressed is never really banished, but merely lies dormant gathering strength or seeps to the surface in disguised forms, we see today an increasing eruption of repressed transcendence. It is taking the form of an interest in meditation, psychic phenomena, yoga, Oriental religions, altered states of consciousness, biofeedback, out-of-body experiences, near-death states. And because it has been generally repressed for so long, this urge to transcendence occasionally takes on bizarre or exaggerated forms, such as black magic, occultism, misuse of psychedelic drugs, and cultic guru worship.

Yet, with all this outbreak of transcendence, most Westerners still have a great deal of difficulty comprehending how it could be that something deep within them actually transcends space and time, how there could be an awareness within them which, because it transcends the individual, is free of personal problems, tensions, and anxieties. So instead of jumping directly into the middle of a discussion of this transpersonal self, I would like by way of introduction to briefly discuss the work of Carl Jung, Freud's most distinguished student. This will supply some necessary background information—information that, in many other cultures, would have been supplied in one form or another to a person from the time of his birth.

Jung began studying with Freud at the beginning of this century, and although Freud had designated Jung as his sole "successor and crown prince," within a decade Jung had broken with Freud over doctrinal disagreements. After that celebrated parting of the ways, the two great men never again spoke to one another. The basis of their mutual incompatibilities stemmed from the fact (mentioned in the first chapter) that any psychological researcher, investigating a particular level of the spectrum, will generally acknowledge as real all levels on and above his own, but will often deny reality to any level deeper than his own. He will proclaim these deeper levels to be pathological, illusory, or nonexistent.

Freud ended up confining his remarkable and courageous investigations to the ego, persona, and shadow. But Jung, while fully acknowledging these upper levels, managed to push his explorations all the way down to the transpersonal bands. Jung was the first major European psychologist to discover and explore significant aspects of the transpersonal realm of human awareness. Freud could not comprehend this, confined as he was to the upper levels, and thus the two men traveled their separate paths.

But what specifically did Jung stumble onto? What did he discover in the very depths of the human soul that pointed unmistakably to a transpersonal realm? What *in* a person could possibly be *beyond* a person? To begin with, Jung had spent a great deal of time studying world mythology—the whole pantheons of Chinese, Egyptian, Amerindian, Greek, Roman, African, and Indian gods and goddesses and demons and divinities, totems and animisms, ancient symbols, images and mythological motifs. What amazed Jung was that these primitive mythological images also appeared regularly and unmistakably *in the dreams and fantasies of modern, civilized Europeans,* the vast majority of whom had never been exposed to these myths (at least, they did not possess the formidable and astonishingly accurate knowledge of mythology displayed in their dreams). This information was not acquired during their lifetimes, and thus, Jung reasoned, in some sense or another, these basic mythological motifs must be innate structures inherited by every member of the human race. These primordial images or archetypes, as Jung called them, are thus common to all people. They belong to no single individual, but are instead transindividual, collective, transcendent.

This is a plausible hypothesis, especially if one carefully examines the reams of meticulously detailed data reported by Jung. Just as, for example, each person possesses one heart, two kidneys, ten fingers, four limbs, and so on, so each person's brain might contain universal *symbolic forms* essentially identical to those of all other normal human brains. The human brain itself is millions of years old, and over that vast expanse of time it necessarily evolved certain basic (and in this sense "mythological") ways of perceiving and grasping reality, just as our hands evolved in special ways to grasp physical objects. These basic imaginative mythological ways of grasping reality are the archetypes, and because every person's basic brain structure is similar, every person may house within him the same basic mythological archetypes. Since they are common to all people by simple virtue of a shared membership in the human race, Jung called this deep layer of the psyche the "collective unconscious." It is, in other words, not individual nor personal, but supra-individual, transpersonal, transcendent. Buried deep in every person's being is the mythology of transcendence, and ignoring this powerful layer can only have the most regrettable consequences.

Parts of the unconscious (corresponding with the persona, ego, and centaur levels) contain *personal* memories, personal wishes and ideas and experiences and potentials. But the deeper realms, the collective unconscious *within you* contains nothing strictly personal whatsoever. Rather, it houses the collective motifs of the entire human race—all the gods and goddesses, divinities and demons, heroes and villains portrayed outwardly by the world's ancient mythologies are contained, in condensed form, in the depths of your own being. Whether we know it or not, according to Jung, they live on and continue to move us deeply in ways both creative and destructive.

The aim of some types of transpersonal band therapy, such as Jung's, is therefore to help us consciously acknowledge, befriend, and utilize these powerful forces instead of being moved by them unconsciously and against our wills. You might, for example, have a "key dream" where the central image is a sphinx, a gorgon, a great serpent, a winged horse, or some other mythological material. Through a little study of ancient mythology, you can easily learn what these mythological images have meant to the human race on the whole, and thereby discover *what these images mean to your own collective unconscious.* By integrating this meaning into your conscious awareness, you are no longer forcibly controlled by it. The depth of your soul thus begins to loosen, and the crusty topsoil of normal egoic or centauric awareness begins to gently break apart to allow a growth of the transcendent, a growth of those processes which transcend your personal life, but which are nevertheless aspects of a deeper self.

Let us examine, in this context of archetypal awareness, just how this shift to a deeper self, a transpersonal self, might occur. As the individual begins to reflect on her life through the eyes of the archetypes and mythological images common to humankind, her awareness may begin to shift to a more universal perspective. She is looking at herself not through her own eyes, which are in some ways prejudiced, but through the eyes of the collective human spirit—a different view indeed! She is no longer exclusively preoccupied with her own personal vantage point. In fact, if this process quickens correctly, her identity, her very self, expands qualitatively to these more or less global dimensions, and her soul becomes saturated with depth. She is no longer exclusively identified with just her ego or centaur, and thus she is no longer suffocated by purely personal problems and dramas. In a sense she can let go of her individual concerns and view them with a creative detachment, realizing that whatever problems her personal self faces, her deeper self transcends them to remain untouched, free, and open. She finds, haltingly at first but then with an ever-increasing certainty, a quiet source of inner strength that persists unperturbed, like the depths of the ocean, even though the surface waves of consciousness are swept with torrents of pain, anxiety, or despair.

The discovery, in one form or another, of this transcendent self is the major aim of all transpersonal band therapies and disciplines. However, the mythological approach we have been discussing thus far is by no means the only path to the transcendent self. To every level of the spectrum there exist numerous different approaches, and individuals may have to experiment somewhat to determine which is best for them. I have dwelt on the mythological as a convenient introduction to the realm of the transpersonal, but the strictly mythological route is a difficult one and usually demands a professional assistant to help guide you through the vast maze of the world's mythologies and your own archetypal layer.

There are simpler approaches to the transcendent self; not necessarily shorter or easier, but much less delicate and complicated. Individuals can undertake these on their own and pursue them under their own initiative. These are the approaches we will now explore.

Notice first of all the broad, distinguishing marks of the transcendent self: it is a center and expanse of awareness which is creatively detached from one's personal mind, body, emotions, thoughts, and feelings. So if you would like to begin to work at intuiting this transcendent self within you that goes beyond you, the you that is not you, then proceed as follows:

Begin with two or three minutes of centaur awareness as described in the last chapter (for the simple reason that you will then be more or less in touch with the centaur level, and that much "closer" to the transpersonal bands beneath it). Then, slowly begin to silently recite the following to yourself, trying to realize as vividly as possible the import of each statement:

I *have* a body, but I am *not* my body. I can see and feel my body, and what can be seen and felt is not the true Seer. My body may be tired or excited, sick or healthy, heavy or light, but that has nothing to do with my inward I. I *have* a body, but I am *not* my body.

I *have* desires, but I am *not* my desires. I can know my desires, and what can be known is not the true Knower. Desires come and go, floating through my awareness, but they do not affect my inward I. I *have* desires but I am *not* desires.

I *have* emotions, but I am *not* my emotions. I can feel and sense my emotions, and what can be felt and sensed is not the true Feeler. Emotions pass through me, but they do not affect my inward I. I *have* emotions but I am *not* emotions.

I *have* thoughts, but I am *not* my thoughts. I can know and intuit my thoughts, and what can be known is not the true Knower. Thoughts come to me and thoughts leave me, but they do not affect my inward I. I *have* thoughts but I am *not* my thoughts.

This done—perhaps several times—one then affirms as concretely as possible: I am what remains, a pure center of awareness, an unmoved witness of all these thoughts, emotions, feelings, and desires.

If you persist at such an exercise, the understanding contained in it will quicken and you might begin to notice fundamental changes in your sense of "self." For example, you might begin intuiting a deep inward sense of freedom, lightness, release, stability. This source, this "center of the cyclone," will retain its lucid stillness even amid the raging winds of anxiety and suffering that might swirl around its center. The discovery of this witnessing center is very much like diving from the calamitous waves on the surface of a stormy ocean to the quiet and secure depths of the bottom. At first you might not get more than a few feet beneath the agitated waves of emotion, but with persistence you may gain the ability to dive fathoms into the quiet depths of your soul, and lying outstretched at the bottom, gaze up in alert but detached fashion at the turmoil that once held you transfixed.

Here we are talking of the transpersonal self or witness—we are not yet discussing pure unity consciousness. In unity consciousness, the transpersonal witness itself collapses into everything witnessed. Before that can occur, however, one must first discover that transpersonal witness, which then acts as an easier "jumping-off point" for unity consciousness. This chapter is devoted to the witness; the next chapter to its "collapse" into Unity. And we find this transpersonal witness by disidentifying with *all* particular objects, mental, emotional, or physical, thereby transcending them.

To the extent that you actually realize that you are not, for example, your anxieties, then your anxieties no longer threaten you. Even if anxiety is present, it no longer overwhelms you because you are no longer exclusively tied to it. You are no longer courting it, fighting it, resisting it, or running from it. In the most radical fashion, anxiety is thoroughly accepted as it is and allowed to move as it will. You have nothing to lose, nothing to gain, by its presence or absence, for you are simply watching it pass by.

Thus, any emotion, sensation, thought, memory, or experience that disturbs you is simply one with which you have exclusively identified yourself, and the ultimate resolution of the disturbance is simply to *dis-identify* with it. You cleanly let all of them drop away by realizing that they are not you—since you can see them, they cannot be the true Seer and Subject. Since they are not your real self, there is no reason whatsoever for you to identify with them, hold on to them, or allow your self to be bound by them.

Slowly, gently, as you pursue this dis-identification "therapy," you may find that your entire *individual* self (persona, ego, centaur), which heretofore you have fought to defend and protect, begins to go transparent and drop away. Not that it literally falls off and you find yourself floating, disembodied, through space. Rather, you begin to feel that what happens to your personal self—your wishes, hopes, desires, hurts—is not a matter of life-or-death seriousness, because there is within you a deeper and more basic self which is not touched by these peripheral fluctuations, these surface waves of grand commotion but feeble substance.

Thus, your personal mind-and-body may be in pain, or humiliation, or fear, but as long as you abide as the witness of these affairs, as if from on high, they no longer threaten *you,* and thus you are no longer moved to manipulate them, wrestle with them, or subdue them. Because you are willing to witness them, to look at them impartially, you are able to transcend them. As St. Thomas put it, "Whatever knows certain things cannot have any of them in its own nature." Thus, if the eye were colored red, it wouldn't be able to perceive red objects. It can see red because it is clear, or "redless." Likewise, if we can but watch or witness our distresses, we prove ourselves thereby to be "distress-less," free of the witnessed turmoil. That within which feels pain is itself pain-less; that which feels fear is fear-less; that which perceives tension is tension-less. To witness these states is to transcend them. They no longer seize you from behind because you look at them up front.

Thus, we can understand why Patanjali, the codifier of yoga in India, said that ignorance is the identification of the Seer with the instruments of seeing. Every time we become exclusively identified with or attached to the persona, ego, or centaur, then anything which threatens their existence or standards seems to threaten our very Self. Thus, every attachment to thoughts, sensations, feelings, or experiences is merely another link in the chain of our own self-enslavement.

In all previous chapters we have spoken of "therapy" as an "expanding" of identity, but now, rather abruptly, we are speaking of dis-identifying. Isn't this contradictory? Actually, these are but two ways of speaking about a single process. Look again at figure 1 and notice, for example, the descent from the persona to the ego level. Two things have happened in this particular descent. One, the individual *identifies* with his shadow. But two, he *dis-identifies* with, or breaks his exclusive attachment to, his persona. His "new" identity, the ego, is thus a synergistic combination of both persona and shadow. Likewise, to descend to the centaur level, a person extends his identity to the body while dis-identifying with the ego *alone*. In each case, not only do we expand to a new and broader identity, we also break an old and narrowed one. In the same way, we "expand" to the broader identity of the transcendent self by gently breaking or letting-go of our narrower identity with the centaur alone. We dis-identify with the centaur, but in the direction of depth and expanse.

Thus, as we begin to touch the transpersonal witness, we begin to let go of our purely personal problems, worries, and concerns. In fact (and this is the entire key to most transpersonal band therapies), we don't even try to solve our problems or distresses, as we surely would and should on the persona, ego, or centaur levels. For our only concern here is to *watch* our particular distresses, to simply and innocently be aware of them, without judging them, avoiding them, dramatizing them, working on them, or justifying them. As a feeling or tendency arises, we witness it. If hatred of that feeling arises, we witness that. If hatred of the hatred arises, then we witness *that*. Nothing is to be done, but if a doing arises, we witness that. Abide as "choiceless awareness" in the midst of all distresses. This is possible only when we understand that none of them constitute our real self. As long as we are attached to them, there will be an effort, however subtle, to manipulate them. Understanding that they are not the center or self, we don't call our distresses names, yell at them, resent them, try to reject them or indulge them. Every move we make to solve a distress simply reinforces the illusion that we *are* that particular distress. Thus, ultimately to try to escape a distress merely perpetuates that distress. What is so upsetting is not the distress itself, but our *attachment* to that distress. We identify with it, and that alone is the real difficulty.

Instead of fighting a distress, we simply assume the innocence of a

detached impartiality toward it. The mystics and sages are fond of liken-
ing this state of witnessing to a mirror. We simply reflect any sensations
or thoughts that arise without clinging to them or pushing them away,
just as a mirror perfectly and impartially reflects whatever passes in front
of it. Says Chuang Tzu, "The perfect person employs the mind as a
mirror. It grasps nothing; it refuses nothing; it receives, but does not
keep."

If you are at all successful in developing this type of detached witnessing (it does take time), you will be able to look upon the events occurring
in your mind-and-body with the very same impartiality that you would
look upon clouds floating through the sky, water rushing in a stream,
rain cascading on a roof, or any other objects in your field of awareness.
In other words, your *relationship* to your mind-and-body becomes the
same as your *relationship* to *all other objects*. Heretofore, you have been
using your mind-and-body as something with which to look at the
world. Thus, you became intimately attached to them and bound to
their limited perspective. You became identified exclusively with them
and thus you were tied and bound to their problems, pains, and distresses. But by persistently looking at them, you realize they are merely
objects of awareness—in fact, objects of the transpersonal witness. "I
have a mind and body and emotions, but I am *not* a mind and body and
emotions."

It is important to affirm that just because a person begins to contact,
or even totally shift to, the transpersonal bands, she does not lose access
to or control over any of the upper levels of the spectrum. Remember
that as an individual descends from an exclusive identity with the persona to a fuller and more accurate identity with her total ego, she does
not lose access to the persona—she is just no longer stuck to it. She can
still don her persona, if, for instance, she chooses to put on a "good
show" or a temporary social facade for practical or decorous purposes.
But she is no longer chronically anchored in that role. Formerly, she
could not drop this facade, either for others or—and here is the problem—herself. Now, however, she can simply use it or not, depending
upon circumstances and her own discretion. If she decides to put on her
"good face," her persona, then she consciously and temporarily checks
her shadow, not showing her negative aspects. She is still capable of
being aware of them, however, and thus she doesn't project them. So the
persona in itself is not maladaptive or problem-generating—unless it's
the only self you have. Thus, what is dissolved when one descends from

the persona level to the ego level is not the shadow or the persona, but the boundary and the battle between them.

Likewise, when you descend to the centaur level from the ego level, you don't destroy the ego or the body, but simply the boundary between them. On the centaur level, you still have access to the ego, the body, the persona, and the shadow; but because you are no longer exclusively identified with one as against the others, all of these elements work in harmony. You have befriended them all and touched each with acceptance. There are no intractable boundaries between them and so no major battles.

In the same way, as you contact the transpersonal self, you still have access to all the levels above it. No longer, however, will you be tied to those levels, bound to them, or limited by them. They become instrumental, not essential. Thus, as a person begins this creative detachment from the exclusive identification with the isolated organism, he in no way ceases caring for his organism. He doesn't stop eating, living, etc. Actually the reverse is the case. One becomes more caring and accepting of the mind-and-body. Since one is no longer *bound* by them, they no longer appear as a freedom-robbing prison. Thus the person's energies are not frozen in a suppressed rage and hatred for his own organism. The organism as a whole becomes a perfectly accepted expression of the transpersonal self.

As we mentioned earlier, from the position of the transcendent witness one begins to view the mind-and-body in the same way one would view any other object of awareness, be it a table, a tree, a dog, a car. This might sound as though we would treat our organism with the disdain that we occasionally show the environment. But it actually works to the other side: we begin to treat all environmental objects as if they were our own self. In fact, this attitude represents the intuition that the world is really one's body and is to be treated as such. It is from this type of transpersonal intuition that the universal compassion so emphasized by the mystics springs. This is a different order of compassion or love than one finds on the persona, ego, or centaur level. At the transpersonal level, we begin to love others not because they love us, affirm us, reflect us, or secure us in our illusions, but because they *are* us. Christ's primary teaching does not mean, "Love your neighbor as you love yourself," but "Love your neighbor *as* your Self." And not just your neighbor, but your whole environment. You begin to care for your surroundings just as you would your own arms and legs. At this level, remember, your relationship to your environment is the same as your relationship to your very own organism.

At the level of the transpersonal witness, the archetypal self, you might also begin to regain a fundamental intuition, an intuition you probably possessed as a child. Namely, that since consciousness fundamentally transcends the separate organism, then (1) it is single, and (2) it is immortal.

Almost every child wonders, at some time or another, "What would I be like if I had different parents?" In other words, the child realizes, in a very innocent and inarticulate fashion, that consciousness itself (that inner Witness or I-ness) is not solely limited by the particular outer forms of mind and body that it animates. Every child seems to sense that he would still be "I" even if he had different parents and a different body. The child knows he would look different and act different, but *he would still be an "I"* ("I have a mind and body and emotions, but *I* am not the mind and body and emotions.") The child asks this question— "Would I still be *me* if I had different parents?"—because he wants the parents to explain his transcendence, the fact that he would still seem to be and feel the same "inner-I-ness" even though he had different parents. The parents have probably long ago forgotten their own transpersonal self, and so cannot give an answer acceptable to the child. But for a moment, most parents are taken aback, and sense that there is something of immense importance here that somehow they just can't quite remember. . . .

Anyone who fundamentally begins to intuit the transpersonal self might realize that there is but *one* Self taking on these different outward forms, for every person has the identical intuition of this *same* I-ness transcending the body. This single Self cleanly transcends the mind and body, and thus is *essentially one and the same in all conscious beings.* Just as a person can walk out of one room and into another, without fundamentally changing his inward feeling of I-ness, so also he would not be fundamentally different if he possessed a different body, with different memories, and different sensations. He is the witness of these objects, but he is not tied to them.

The insight that the transcendent self passes beyond the individual organism also carries with it an intuition of immortality. Most people harbor the inward feeling that they are immortal. They cannot imagine their own nonexistence. Nobody can! But the average person, because he exists only as the centaur, ego, or persona, falsely imagines, and deeply wishes, that his *individual* self will live forever. It is *not* true that the mind, ego, or body is immortal. They, like all composites, will die. They are dying now, and not one of them will survive eternally. Reincarnation does not mean that your ego moves through successive existences, but that the transcendent self is the "one and only transmigrant," as Shankara himself put it.

In a certain sense, therefore, we have to "die" to our false, separate self in order to awaken to our immortal and transcendent self. Thus the famous paradox, "If you die before you die, then when you die, you won't die." And the sayings of the mystics that "No one gets as much of God as the one who is thoroughly dead." This is why so many people who consistently practice some form of transpersonal "therapy" report that they no longer really fear death.

Perhaps we can approach this fundamental insight of the mystics and sages—that there is but *one* immortal Self common in and to us all—in yet another way. Perhaps you, like most people, feel that you are basically the same person you were yesterday. You probably also feel that you are *fundamentally* the same person you were a year ago. Indeed, you still seem to be the *same* you as far back as you can remember. Put it another way: you never remember a time when you weren't you. In other words, *something* in you seems to remain untouched by the passage of time. But surely your body is not the same as it was even a year ago. Surely also your sensations are different today than in the past. Surely, too, your memories are on the whole different today than a decade ago. Your mind, your body, your feelings—*all* have changed with time. But something has not changed, and you know that something has not changed. Something feels the same. What is that?

This time a year ago you had different concerns and basically different problems. Your immediate experiences were different, and so were your thoughts. All of these have vanished, but something in you remains. Go one step further. What if you moved to a completely different country, with new friends, new surroundings, new experiences, new thoughts. You would still have that basic inner feeling of I-ness. Further yet, what if you right now forgot the first ten years, or fifteen years, or twenty years of your life? You would still feel that same inner I-ness, would you not? If right now you just temporarily forget *everything* that happened in your past, and just feel that pure inner I-ness—has *anything* really changed?

There is, in short, something within you—that deep inward sense of I-ness—that is *not* memory, thoughts, mind, body, experience, surroundings, feelings, conflicts, sensations, or moods. For *all* of these have changed and can change without substantially affecting that inner I-ness. *That* is what remains untouched by the flight of time—and that is the transpersonal witness and self.

Is it then so very difficult to realize that *every* conscious being has that *same* inner I-ness? And that, therefore, the overall number of transcendent I's is but *one*? We have already surmised that if you had a different body you would still basically feel the same I-ness—but that is already the very same way every other person feels right now. Isn't it just as easy to say there is but one single I-ness or Self taking on different views, different memories, different feelings and sensations?

And not just at this time, but at all times, past and future. Since you undoubtedly feel (even though your memory, mind, and body are different) that you are the same person of twenty years ago (not the same ego or body, but the same I-ness), couldn't you also be the same I-ness of two-hundred years ago? If I-ness isn't dependent upon memories and mind and body, what difference would it make? In the words of physicist Schroedinger, "It is not possible that this unity of knowledge, feeling and choice which you call *your own* should have sprung into being from nothingness at a given moment not so long ago; rather this knowledge, feeling and choice are essentially eternal and unchangeable and numerically *one* in all men, nay in all sensitive beings. The conditions for your existence are almost as old as the rocks. For thousands of years men have striven and suffered and begotten and women have brought forth in pain. A hundred years ago, perhaps, another man sat on this spot; like you he gazed with awe and yearning in his heart at the dying light on the glaciers. Like you he was begotten of man and born of woman. He felt pain and brief joy as you do. *Was* he someone else? Was it not you yourself?"

Ah, we say, that couldn't have been me, because I can't remember what happened then. But that is to make the mistake of identifying I-ness with memories, and we just saw that I-ness is not memory but the witness of memory. Besides, you probably can't even remember what happened to you last month, but you are still I-ness. So what if you can't remember what happened last century? You are still that transcendent I-ness, and that I—there is only one in the whole cosmos—is the same I which awakens in every newborn being, the same I which looked out from our ancestors and will look out from our descendants—one and the same I. We feel they are different only because we make the error of identifying the inward and transpersonal I-ness with the outward and individual memory, mind, and body, which indeed are different.

But as for that inward I . . . indeed, what is that? It was not born with your body, nor will it perish upon death. It does not recognize time nor cater to its distresses. It is without color, without shape, without form, without size, and yet it beholds the entire majesty before your own eyes. It sees the sun, clouds, stars and moon, but cannot itself be seen. It hears the birds, the crickets, the singing waterfall, but cannot itself be heard. It grasps the fallen leaf, the crusted rock, the knotted branch, but cannot itself be grasped.

You needn't try to see your transcendent self, which is not possible anyway. Can your eye see itself? You need only begin by persistently dropping your false identifications with your memories, mind, body, emotions, and thoughts. And this dropping entails nothing by way of superhuman effort or theoretical comprehension. All that is required, primarily, is but one understanding: *whatever you can see cannot be the Seer.* *Everything* you know about yourself is precisely *not* your Self, the Knower, the inner I-ness that can neither be perceived, defined, or made an *object* of any sort. Bondage is nothing but the mis-identification of the Seer with all these things which can be *seen*. And liberation begins with the simple reversal of this mistake.

Any time you identify with a problem, an anxiety, a mental state, a memory, a desire, a bodily sensation or emotion—you are throwing yourself into bondage, limitation, fear, constriction, and ultimately death. These all can be seen and thus are not the Seer. On the other hand, to continuously abide as the Seer, the Witness, the Self, is to step *aside* from limitations and problems, and then finally to step *out* of them.

This is a simple but arduous practice, yet its results constitute nothing less than liberation in this life, for the transcendent self is everywhere acknowledged as a ray of the Divine. In principle, your transcendent self is of one nature with God (however you might wish to conceive it). For it is finally, ultimately, profoundly, God alone who looks through your eyes, listens with your ears, and speaks with your tongue. How else could St. Clement maintain that he who knows himself knows God?

This, then, is the message of Jung; and more, of the saints, sages, and mystics, whether Amerindian, Taoist, Hindu, Islamic, Buddhist, or Christian: At the bottom of your soul is the soul of humanity itself, but a divine, transcendent soul, leading from bondage to liberation, from enchantment to awakening, from time to eternity, from death to immortality.

RECOMMENDATIONS

There are so many aspects of the transpersonal bands, and so many different approaches, we will take them in groups.

For the works of C. G. Jung, Joseph Campbell's *The Portable Jung* (New York: Viking, 1972) is an excellent anthology of Jung's own writings, and is highly recommended. For an overall introduction to Jung's analytical psychology, see Bennet, E. A., *What Jung Really Said* (New York: Dutton, 1966). The serious student is directed to an outstanding comparison of Freud's and Jung's systems: Lilliane Frey-Rohn, *From Freud to Jung* (New York: Delta, 1974). For a practical, do-it-yourself, but extremely effective approach to a Jungian-type therapy, I highly recommend Ira Progoff's *At a Journal Workshop* (New York: Dialogue House, 1975).

For Maslow's groundbreaking studies of the transpersonal, see his *Toward a Psychology of Being* (New York: Van Nostrand, 1968) and *The Farther Reaches of Human Nature* (New York: Viking, 1971). For those interested in traditional psychologies, see C. Tart (ed.), *Transpersonal Psychologies* (New York: Harpers, 1975). Well-rounded anthologies include J. White, *The Highest State of Consciousness* (New York: Anchor, 1972); J. Welwood, *Meeting of the Ways* (New York: Schocken, 1979); R. Walsh and F. Vaughan, *Beyond Ego* (Los Angeles: Tarcher, 1979). Frances Vaughan has also written a valuable book, *Awakening Intuition* (New York: Anchor, 1979), about just that. My own books, *The Spectrum of Consciousness* (Wheaton: Quest, 1977), and *The Atman Project* (Wheaton: Quest, 1980) try to put much of this material in perspective. If you are a psychiatrist, and would appreciate a more cautious approach, try S. Dean (ed.), *Psychiatry and Mysticism* (Chicago: Nelson Hall, 1975).

Psychosynthesis represents a sound and effective approach to the transcendent self in no uncertain terms; the book *Psychosynthesis* (New York: Viking, 1965), by its founder Roberto Assagioli, is an encompassing introduction. The exercise in dis-identification given in this chapter was adapted from that book. For important data from psychedelic research, see S. Grof, *Realms of the Human Unconscious* (New York: Viking, 1975).

For the transcendent unity of religions and the perennial philosophy in general—see F. Schuon, *The Transcendent Unity of Religions* (New York: Harper, 1975). Huston Smith's *The Forgotten Truth* (New York: Harper, 1976) is the best introduction to the field for the general reader.

As for the meditation and the transpersonal, a useful anthology is J. White, *What Is Meditation?* (New York: Anchor, 1972). But I should say here that many approaches to the transpersonal bands also aim through these bands to the level of unity consciousness, and so I am rather arbitrarily dividing my recommendations between those to list here and those to include in the next chapter. In general, those listed here usually establish, as a type of "halfway" house, a base of awareness in the transpersonal bands, and then proceed to the level of unity consciousness from there (*if* they proceed at all).

The transpersonal bands are actually composed of several sublevels, and different types of meditation seem to address these different sublevels. For the kundalini division, see J. White (ed.), *Kundalini, Evolution, and Enlightenment* (New York: Anchor, 1979). For the subtler aspects (known as nada or shabd), the reader is directed to any of the works of Kirpal Singh.

Because Transcendental Meditation is simple, effective, and, most important, readily accessible, it would be one of my first recommendations for an introduction to this type of meditation. My final recommendations for meditation in general are reserved for the next chapter.

10

The Ultimate State of Consciousness

There is neither creation nor destruction,
Neither destiny nor free-will;
Neither path nor achievement;
This is the final truth.

—SRI RAMANA MAHARSHI

SINCE UNITY CONSCIOUSNESS is of the timeless moment, it is entirely present now. And obviously, there is no way to reach now. There is no way to *arrive* at that which already is. Hence, as Ramana suggests, there is no path to unity consciousness, and this he proclaims the final truth.

This seems an odd or at least a frustrating conclusion, especially since we have just spent so much time exploring some of the practical ways we could contact the other levels of the spectrum. In the past few chapters, we have seen that there are certain practices, techniques, and disciplines which could facilitate descent to any of the other levels. Now the reason we could contact these levels is that they are *partial*—i.e., less than comprehensive—states of consciousness. They are *different* from other levels and therefore they can be developed to the exclusion of all others. They have boundaries, either subtle or gross, and thus can be *selectively* worked on.

But the situation is somewhat different with the "level" of unity consciousness, because unity consciousness is not a partial state. Instead, it is all-inclusive in the most radical way, much as a mirror equally includes all the objects it reflects. Unity consciousness is not a state different or apart from other states, but the condition and true nature of *all* states.

If it were different from any state (for example, if it were different from your awareness right now), then that would imply it had a boundary, that it had something to separate it from your present awareness. But unity consciousness has no boundaries, so there is nothing to separate it from anything. Enlightenment flashes clear in this moment, and this moment, and this.

Perhaps a simple analogy will help explain this point. The different levels of the spectrum are something like the various waves of the ocean—each wave is certainly different from all others. Some waves, near the shore, are strong and powerful; while others, farther out, are weaker and less powerful. But each wave is still different from all the others, and if you were surfing you could select a particular wave, catch it, ride it, and work it according to your ability. You couldn't do any of this if the waves weren't different. Each level of the spectrum is like a particular wave, and thus we can "catch" any of them with the right technique and enough practice.

Unity consciousness, however, is not so much a particular wave as it is the *water* itself. And there is no boundary, no difference, no separation between water and any of the waves. That is, the water is equally present in *all* waves, in the sense that no wave is wetter than another.

So if you are looking for "wetness" itself—the *condition* of all waves—nothing whatsoever will be gained by jumping from one wave to another. In fact, there is much to lose, for as long as you are wave-jumping in search of wetness, you obviously will never discover that wetness exists in its purity on whatever wave you're riding now. Seeking unity consciousness is like jumping from one wave of experience to another in search of water. And that is why "there is neither path nor achievement." The great Zen master Hakuin seemed to have just this analogy in mind when he wrote:

> Not knowing how near Truth is,
> People seek it far away—what a pity!
> They are like he who, in the midst of water,
> Cries in thirst so imploringly.

So perhaps we can begin to see why, strictly speaking, there is no path to unity consciousness. Unity consciousness is not a particular experience among other experiences, not a big experience opposed to a small experience, not one wave instead of another. Rather, it is every wave of present experience just as it is. And how can you contact present experience? There is nothing but present experience, and there is definitely no path to that which always is. There is no path to wetness if you're already standing shoulder-deep in water.

It is for all these reasons that the true sages proclaim there is no path to the Absolute, no way to *gain* unity consciousness. Says Shankara, a Hindu, "As Brahman constitutes a person's Self it is not something to be attained by that person." Says Huang Po, a Buddhist, "That there is nothing to be attained is not idle talk; it is the truth." Says Eckhart, a Christian, "Thou shalt know God without image and without means (without path)." Says Krishnamurti, a modern sage, "The real is near, you do not have to search for it; and a man who seeks truth will never find it."

As Eckhart put it, there are *no means* to the ultimate, no techniques, no paths, and this is only because it is its nature to be omnipresent, present everywhere and everywhen. Our difficulty, it seems, is the same as that of the individual who jumps from wave to wave in search of wetness. We won't hold still long enough to understand our present condition. And in always looking elsewhere, we are actually *moving away* from the answer, in the sense that if we are always looking beyond, the essential understanding of the present condition will not unfold. Our very search, our own desire, forestalls the discovery. In short, we are always trying to move away from present experience, whereas in fact it is *this present experience* which always holds the key to our search. We are not really searching for the answer—we are fleeing it.

But does this mean that we are to do nothing? That we are to stop moving away from the present? That we are to try to fully contact the now? That seems reasonable enough, until we examine it more closely. Even doing nothing is utterly beside the point, for *why* do we want to do nothing? Isn't that just another attempt to *move away* from this present wave of experience in search of a wetter one? Whether we try to do, or try not to do, *we still have to make a move*—and thus miss the point in the very first step.

This, then, is the grand paradox of unity consciousness. You can't really do anything to get it—I think that is at least theoretically clear. And yet it is even more obvious that if we don't do something, we'll remain just as we are. Zen Master Ma-tsu put it bluntly, "In the Tao there is nothing to discipline oneself in. If there is any discipline in it, the completion of such discipline means the destruction of the Tao. But if there is no discipline whatever in the Tao, one remains an ignoramus."

And so we arrive at an essential point of the major mystical traditions, namely, that *special conditions* are appropriate (but not necessary) for the actualization of unity consciousness. And further, these conditions do not *lead* to unity consciousness—they are themselves an *expression* of unity consciousness. They are a formal, ritual embodiment and enjoyment of original enlightenment.

Zen Buddhism, for instance, has a beautiful saying: *honsho-myoshu,* which means "original enlightenment is wondrous practice." Unity consciousness is not a *future* state which *results* from some practice, because that would imply that unity consciousness has a *beginning* in time, that it doesn't exist now but will exist tomorrow. That would make unity consciousness a strictly temporal state, which is not acceptable at all, for unity consciousness is present eternally.

That unity consciousness is always present is our *honsho,* our "original enlightenment," original not because it occurred in ancient times past, but because it is the *origin* and ground of this instant. Enlightenment is the origin of the present form. *Myoshu,* spiritual practice, is the movement or activity of this origin; it is the appropriate function of origin-al enlightenment.

Honsho-myoshu therefore means that true spiritual practice springs *from,* but not *toward,* enlightenment. Our practice does not lead *to* unity consciousness, our practice *is* unity consciousness from the beginning—from, in fact, all time. In the words of Suzuki Roshi:

> If our practice is only a means to attain enlightenment, there is actually no way to attain it. Enlightenment is not some good feeling or some particular state of mind. The state of mind that exists when you sit [in zazen practice] is, itself, enlightenment. In this posture there is no need to talk about the right state of mind. You already have it.

And is this really any different from the esoteric Christian doctrine that in true prayer, it is not that you are trying to reach God, but that it is God who is praying to himself? "Console thyself; thou wouldst not seek Me if thou hadst not already found." Thus, by all accounts, our spiritual practice is itself already the goal. The end and the means, the way and the destination, the alpha and omega, are one.

But this raises yet another question. Why, then, should we practice at all if we already have Buddha-nature or original enlightenment or the inner Christ? Well, we could say, "Why not?" But the real point is that the taking up of the special conditions of spiritual practice is an appropriate expression of unity consciousness. A priceless jewel is of no earthly value whatsoever unless you can employ it, express it, manifest it. Likewise, an appropriate use of original, spiritual enlightenment is spiritual activity in its fullest sphere. Even if, in our spiritual practice, it appears we are trying to *attain* enlightenment, we are actually only *expressing* it. If we take up zazen, for instance, then deep within we are doing so not to become Buddhas but to behave like the Buddhas we already are. To quote Suzuki Roshi once again:

> The understanding passed down from Buddha to our time is that when you start zazen, there is enlightenment without any preparation. Whether you practice zazen or not, you have Buddha nature. Because you have it, there is enlightenment in your practice. If originally we have Buddha nature, the reason we practice zazen is that we must behave like Buddha. Our way is not to sit to acquire something; it is to express our true nature. That is our practice. Zazen practice is the direct expression of our true nature. Strictly speaking, for a human being, there is no other practice than this practice; there is no other way of life than this way of life.

Suzuki Roshi doesn't mean that Buddhism *per se* is the only life, but that unity consciousness or "Big Mind" is the only life. And because of *honsho-myoshu,* moment-to-moment practice as the joyful and grateful expression of original enlightenment is the only way to live. From this side, there is indeed no other way to live, but, as an alternative, only numerous ways to suffer.

If we understand *honsho-myoshu,* then everything we do *is* practice, is an expression of original enlightenment. Every act springs from eternity, from no-boundary, and, just as it is, is a perfect and unobstructed expression of the All. Everything we do becomes our practice, our prayer—not just zazen, chanting, the sacraments, mantra meditation, sutra recitation or Bible readings—but everything, from washing dishes to doing income taxes. And not in the sense that we wash dishes and think of original enlightenment, but because washing dishes is itself original enlightenment.

So we begin any "therapy" aimed at the level of unity consciousness by assuming special conditions of spiritual practice. It might be zazen, or mantra meditation, or devotion to God through Christ or guru, or special visualization procedures. It is impossible, in the space of a short chapter, to outline even one of these spiritual practices, and so readers will have to rely on the recommended readings at the end of this chapter, and pursue these matters on their own. What I intend to do is provide a brief preview of some of the insights and changes that might occur to you as you proceed with a spiritual practice. This may give you at least a feel for what some of these practices are like, and thus help you decide if they are worth pursuing in your case.

As individuals take up the special conditions of a spiritual practice, they will begin to realize, with increasing certainty and clarity, an exasperating but unmistakable fact: nobody wants unity consciousness. At all times we are, in truth, *resisting* unity consciousness, avoiding God, fighting the Tao. It is certain that we are always wave-jumping, that we are always resisting the present wave of experience. But unity consciousness and the present are one and the same thing. To resist one is to resist the other. In theological terms, we are always resisting God's presence, which is nothing but the full present in all its forms. If there is some aspect of life that you dislike, there is some aspect of unity consciousness that you are resisting. Thus we actively, if secretly, deny and resist unity consciousness. The understanding of this secret resistance is the ultimate key to enlightenment.

But we should notice that this is not the first time we have seen some form of *resistance*. In fact, every major level of the spectrum is actually constituted by a particular mode of resistance. When we discussed the descent from the persona level to the ego level, the first thing we encountered was resistance to the shadow. This is why Freud, master investigator of the shadow, stated, "The whole of psychoanalytic theory is in fact built up on the perception of the *resistance* exerted by the patient when we try to make him conscious of his unconscious." In our own exploration of the shadow, we saw this resistance pop up everywhere. We saw that an individual may resist any impulse or information that is unacceptable to her self-image. This resisted material then becomes part of her shadow, leaving the individual with nothing but a symptom in its place. The individual then resists (with basically the same resistance) her symptom. She fights her symptom of anxiety, phobia, or whatever just as she once fought her shadow. Further, she will also resist (again, the same resistance) any person onto whom she might project her own shadow. She then treats people as symptoms.

The perplexing thing—especially to the individual caught in this resistance—is that she (as persona) honestly doesn't think she's resisting. She is totally unaware of it. On the surface, she thinks that if she had her way, she wouldn't suffer, she wouldn't get depressed, tense, or otherwise symptomatic. But that's only true of half of her, for the alienated half of her (the shadow) loves to inflict suffering—on her! So she hurts herself without knowing it. And because she does not know it, she cannot stop. She produces her own symptoms but won't admit it, and thus she ends up defending her suffering. Until she sees her own resistance to her shadow, no progress whatsoever is gained, for she will continue to resist and therefore sabotage any effort at growth.

So the first and most difficult task of the persona-level therapist is to help the individual understand and work through her resistance to her shadow. The therapist doesn't try to get rid of the resistances, by-pass them, or ignore them. Instead the therapist helps the individual see how, and secondarily why, she is resisting her own shadow. Once the person sees that she is, in concrete fact, resisting aspects of herself—and this is really the whole crux of her difficulty—then the person is in a position to gently lower her resistance and begin to touch her shadow, not avoid it, resist it, or repress it. If, however, the individual tried to directly contact the shadow first, without taking into account her resistances, then she would simply redouble her efforts to resist and expel the shadow, since she has ignored the very root cause of the problem.

In psychoanalysis, for example, which embodies a very consistent approach to the shadow, the person will be asked to take up free association. He will be instructed to say anything and everything that comes into his mind, no matter how outrageous, inconsequential, or even silly it seems. The person will begin, and ideas will start to flow in chains of associations, remembrances, and fantasies. But, rather suddenly, he will invariably hit some sort of snarl. He might go blank, or perhaps get embarrassed, or simply freeze. In starting to free associate, he lowered his resistances, his chronic censorship over his thoughts, and in a matter of minutes under this free and unguarded atmosphere, a shadow idea or impulse has come naturally to the surface, an idea or impulse that he heretofore has warded-off and resisted. As soon as the shadow thought starts to pop up, the individual goes blank in defense. He resists it and thus halts the free flow of associations.

The therapist will point this out. He will not confront the person with the shadow thought, but merely begin by exploring the person's feelings of resistance to some of his own thoughts. By persistently exploring this resistance in all its forms, the therapist will help the individual to regain his ability to freely range through all of his own thoughts, past, present, and future, without any resistance. Eventually the individual will no longer resist his own impulses and ideas, his own shadow, and thus will have developed a more accurate and acceptable self-image.

That was the first type of resistance that we discovered. The persona resists the shadow, and thus prevents the discovery and emergence of the accurate ego. And as we move down to the next major level of the spectrum, we find a resistance displayed by the ego itself. It is the ego's *resistance to the feeling-attention of the centaur.* Part of this resistance is an inability to maintain true *present-centered* awareness (or feeling-attention) for any length of time. Because centauric awareness is grounded in the passing present, the ego's resistance to the centaur is a resistance to the immediate here and now.

Since it operates basically in time, scanning the past and pressing the future, thinking itself tends to be a resistance to the centaur. In ego therapies, one works with resistances in and to the thought process. In centauric therapies, thought itself is a resistance. In fact, from the deeper view of the centaur level, even the therapeutic technique employed on the ego level is a form of resistance. This is why Fritz Perls, the centaur-level therapist par excellence, could state, "As avoidance [resistance] is assumed to be the central symptom of nervous disorders, I have replaced the method of free association or flight of ideas by that antidote of avoidance—concentration." And concentration on what? Nothing but the immediate present in all its forms and the bodymind awareness which discloses it. Perls soon abandoned the somewhat misleading term "concentration" and replaced it with "awareness of the here and now," and, according to Perls, it is the avoidance or resistance of the centauric here and now that constitutes most pathologies.

Thus, in centaur therapies such as Gestalt, the individual is not asked to let her thoughts run as they please, but rather to suspend "mental chatter" and focus awareness on the immediate here and now. The therapist will watch—not for blocks *in* thought—but for any flight from present awareness *into* thought. The therapist will point out this resistance or avoidance of the here and now to the person, until the person herself understands how she avoids the centaur by escaping into the ego. In ego-level therapy a person will be encouraged to explore her past; in centaur-level therapy, she will be prevented from it. A different type of resistance is operative in each case, and different techniques have evolved to handle them, each technique being valid and appropriate on its own level.

So we are starting to see how each level of the spectrum is marked, among numerous other things, by different modes of resistance or avoidance. On the persona level, we resisted unity with the shadow in all its forms. On the ego level, we resisted unity with the centaur and all its qualities. And finally, as we will now see, on the centaur level itself (and extending into the transpersonal bands) we find the ultimate and primordial resistance—to unity consciousness.

We have also seen how each different resistance resulted in a person's seeing different aspects of himself *as if* they were "objects out there." The shadow appeared as an alien object out there. The body appeared as a foreign object down there. In the same way, the very root resistance, at the base of the spectrum, also results in seeing some aspects of one's self as if they were "objects out there." But at this level, pervasive as it is, these external objects constitute nothing other than the whole environment itself (whether that environment be gross, subtle, personal, or transpersonal). The trees, the stars, the sun and the moon—these "environmental objects" are just as much a part of our real self as the shadow is of our egoic self and the body is of our centauric self.

This primal resistance results in what we ordinarily call *perception.* That is to say, we perceive all sorts of objects as if they were separate from us. And we resist, we actually fight, the awareness of unity with all these perceived objects, just as we once fought unity with the shadow and unity with the whole-bodied centaur. We fight, in short, unity consciousness.

Thus we are brought back to our major point: through assuming appropriate spiritual practices, we start to learn just *how* we resist unity consciousness. Spiritual practice forces this fundamental resistance to surface in our awareness. We begin to see that we don't really want unity consciousness, but that we are always avoiding it. *But that itself is the crucial insight,* just as the understanding of our resistances on every other level was the pivotal insight. To see our resistance to unity consciousness is to be able, for the first time, to deal with it and finally to drop it—thus removing the secret obstacle to our own liberation.

How do these special conditions of spiritual practice reveal to us our resistance to unity consciousness? What, after all, is so special about them? Of the infinite number of activities that we could pursue, why do the ones called "spiritual" work, if we may put it so pragmatically? What is so unique about zazen, or deep contemplation, or devotion to God or guru? Why are they effective? If we can start to understand this, we will have gone a long way in deciphering the paradox of the great liberation.

To begin with, notice that this is really not the first time we have run up against *special conditions*. Like the resistances, we have seen them before under different names. We have seen in the last three chapters that the therapies of each and every level impose special conditions upon the individual. Each different therapy has its own particular practices and special techniques that it imposes on the individual who seeks that level of growth. Without these special conditions, nothing whatsoever would result—except stalemate. These conditions are obviously different for each level. But what is it that they all have in common that allows them to be effective? In other words, let us ask first, why do *any* of these special conditions work?

The answer seems to be that *each type of condition frustrates a type of resistance*. A few short examples will clarify this. We have just noticed that psychoanalysis, which deals primarily with the descent from persona to ego, uses the special condition of free association. Now the ego can free associate with little difficulty, for there are few thoughts or wishes that are totally unacceptable to an accurate ego. The persona, however, can free associate only with the greatest difficulty, because the moment it relaxes its chronic censorship, unwanted and unacceptable thoughts spring to the surface. Free association thus proceeds at best in halts and spurts. The therapist is trained to recognize these blocks as signs of resistance, and to point them out to the individual. Because the individual is directed to assume the special condition, his resistances show up very easily. Further, since he has to keep trying to free associate, keep resuming the special condition, his resistances are slowly frustrated. You cannot resist *and* free associate at the same time. The moment the individual can easily maintain the special condition of unobstructed free association, the therapy is greatly facilitated.

The same factor is at work in the special conditions of centaur-level therapy. For instance, a person might be told to drop all thoughts of yesterday and tomorrow and pay strict feeling-attention to the immediate here and now, the *nunc fluens,* the passing present of existential awareness. This is precisely the special condition. This condition is something the total organism can do with relative ease, but even the accurate ego cannot, for the ego is built upon time, upon successive glances to the past and future, and it withers under the light of present awareness. So the ego will resist the passing present—it will fight the special conditions and always be floating into thoughts of yesterday and tomorrow. The therapist (as always) gently enforces the conditions, and thus frustrates the resistances to this level, the movements away from the immediate, passing present. Without these conditions the individual might never even know she was resisting.

So the special conditions (of each level) *show your resistances and at the same time frustrate them.* Actually, they show you your resistances *by* frustrating them. If your resistances weren't frustrated, you probably wouldn't even suspect their existence. You would continue their secret exercise, thus sabotaging growth. Further, by frustrating your resistances, the conditions allow you to realize a deeper state of no-resistance. In fact, the conditions of any one level are actually what a person on the next deepest level can do. That is, *the special "therapeutic" conditions of any level are one or more of the actual characteristics of the level beneath it.* By assuming the characteristics of the deeper level as the special conditions of your *present practice,* your resistance to that deeper level is exposed, frustrated, and undermined, thus returning you to the deeper level itself.

So we now return to the primal resistance itself, which the special conditions of all true spiritual practices expose and then frustrate, undermine, and dissolve. It is this primal resistance to unity consciousness that we must approach, and not unity consciousness itself. For until you see precisely how you resist unity consciousness, all your efforts to "achieve" it will be in vain, because what you are trying to achieve is also what you are unconsciously resisting and trying to prevent. We secretly resist unity consciousness, we covertly manufacture the "symptoms" of nonenlightenment, just as we secretly produced all our other symptoms on the different levels of the spectrum. What on the surface we fervently desire, in the depths we successfully prevent. And this resistance is our real difficulty. Thus, we won't move *toward* unity consciousness, we will simply understand how we are always moving *away* from it. And that understanding itself might allow a glimpse of unity consciousness, *for that which sees resistance is itself free of resistance.*

The primal resistance, like all other resistances operating throughout the spectrum, is not something that happens to you, nor is it something that happened in the past, nor is it something that occurs without your consent. Rather, it is a present activity, something you are doing without realizing it. And it is this primal activity which tends to block unity consciousness. Put simply, *it is a global unwillingness to look upon everything, as it is, now.* Put concretely, there is something that you won't look at in this present.

On the whole, there exists a global resistance to and nonacceptance of the entire quality of present experience—not just resistance to a particular present experience or some defined and evident aspect of present experience, but the global present in all its dimensions. As we will see, this is not a resistance to the passing present, the *nunc fluens* of the centaur level, but a resistance to the eternal present, the *nunc stans* that is unity consciousness.

Because of its global nature, this resistance is not really something you can clearly perceive and think about. It is rather something very subtle. Wild and dramatic resistances occur mostly on the upper levels, and at the base of the spectrum, this primal resistance is subtle and diffuse. But most of us can inwardly feel and intuit it. Somehow we just don't seem to completely accept the total present state—there is a tiny inward tension that seems to push us away from the global present. Thus we won't allow our awareness to rest naturally on all that is, now. *We tend to look away.*

There is, then, this global unwillingness to look upon everything, as a whole, as it is, just as it is, now. We tend to look away, to withdraw awareness from *what is,* to avoid the present in all its forms. And because we tend to *look* away, we tend to *move* away. With this subtle resistance, this looking-and-moving away, we seem to block unity consciousness; we seem to "lose" our true nature.

This "loss" of unity consciousness throws us into a world of boundaries, space, time, suffering, and mortality. Yet as we move through this world of boundaries and battles, we are motivated basically by one thing: the desire to recapture unity consciousness, to discover once again the territory of no-boundary. All our desires, wants, intentions, and wishes are ultimately "substitute gratifications" for unity consciousness—but only half satisfying, and therefore half frustrating.

So although the only thing a person fundamentally wants is unity consciousness, the only thing she is ever doing is resisting it. We are always looking for unity consciousness, but in a way that always prevents the discovery: we look for unity consciousness by moving away from the present. We imagine that somehow this present is not quite right, is not quite it, and hence we will not globally rest in this present, but start instead to *move away* from it toward what we imagine will be a new and better present. We begin, in other words, to wave-jump. We begin moving in space and time to secure for ourselves an ultimate wave, the wave that will finally quench our thirst, that will finally give us "wetness." Looking for wetness on the next wave of experience, we always miss it on our present wave. To search forever is to miss it forever.

The problem is that, in order to resist the present wave of experience, you have to separate yourself from it. To *move away* from present experience implies that you and present experience are two different things.

By continually trying to move away from now, you continually reinforce the illusion that you are outside the now. By trying to move away from the present world, it appears that you are separate from that world. In just this way we erect the primary boundary between our self on the one hand and our world on the other. This is why we said earlier that the perception of an objective world "out there" is a resistance to, and thus separation from, our present experience.

To move away from now is to separate yourself from unity consciousness, and thus to begin the evolution of the spectrum. That "first cause" of which we spoke so mysteriously in Chapter Six is nothing but this *moving away,* which is embodied in the primary boundary. That is why we said, "The primary boundary, this perpetually active first cause, is *our* going in *this* moment." It is a simple looking and moving away. The moment we resist the one world of present experience, we necessarily divide that world. We divide it into an *inside* experience, which we feel as the seer, experiencer, and actor, versus an *outside* experience, which we feel as the seen, experienced, and acted upon. Our world is split in two, and a boundary, an illusory boundary, is placed between you, the experiencer, and it, the experienced. The evolution of the spectrum has started; the war of the opposites has begun.

Our world is also split in yet another basic way. To continually move away from the global present implies that there is a future which will accept this movement. We move *away* because we imagine there is another time to which we *can* move. To move away is thus nothing more than to move in time—in fact, it is to create time. For by moving away from the timeless and present experience (or rather, by trying to move away), we generate the illusion that experience itself likewise moves past us. By our resisting the eternal and global present, it is reduced to the *passing* present. Experiences then seem to pass by us, one by one in a linear way—but only because we are running past them in a flight from now. (This, as we earlier saw, is the fear of death, the fear of having no future, the fear of *not being able to move away.*)

As we try to move away from the present world, that world appears to move *past* us. The eternal present thus appears bounded, constricted, limited. It is sandwiched on the one side by all the experiences we have run past, and on the other side by all the future moments we are trying to run into. Thus, to move away is to create a before and after, a point of departure in the past *from* which we move and a port of destiny in the future *to* which we move. Our present is reduced to the moving itself, the quiet running away. Our moments pass.

Thus, from all sides, to move away is to separate ourselves from present experience and to project ourselves into time, history, destiny, and death. This, then, is our primal resistance—the unwillingness to look upon all experience, as a whole, as it is, now; and the attempt, instead, to globally move away. It is this global resistance that the special conditions of spiritual practice uncover and then frustrate. As a person assumes the conditions, he starts to realize that he is always *moving away* from the global present. He begins to see that by always moving away, he is merely resisting and preventing unity consciousness—or God's will, the flow of Tao, the love for Guru, or original enlightenment. By any other name, he resists his present. He looks away. He moves away. He therefore suffers.

But, in a sense, he makes progress. He starts to *see* his primal resistance, and thus to relax it. As with all other therapies, this is the "honeymoon" period. He is relatively happy; he is secure in his practice; he feels there is ultimately hope for liberation. He might even get as far as the transpersonal witness (described in the last chapter). Because he starts to see his primal resistance, he starts to understand his enemy. He knows what has to be destroyed. He has to surrender this constant moving away.

Which brings him to disaster. And an abrupt end of the honeymoon. For how on earth can he *stop* moving away? He sees, for instance, that he is at this moment trying to move away from now. So he decides to try to stop that movement away from now. But that action of stopping is itself nothing but another move. To try not to move away is still to make a move. It still requires a future moment in which this stopping might occur. Instead of stopping his moving away, he is merely moving away from moving away. In place of a gross resistance, he has the same resistance on a subtler level.

Approach it from a slightly different angle: he might try to stop resisting the now by attempting to be fully aware of *this* eternal present, exactly as it is. But trying to be aware of this present requires a future present in which this awareness might occur. So he is still *moving away* from now, even in trying not to. For the only present you can *grasp* is the passing present—and that is precisely the therapeutic technique of the centaur level. But at this deepest level, the level of unity consciousness, we are concerned with the eternal present, not the passing present, and to try to grasp or seek the eternal present results only in finding a series of passing presents. To concentrate on the passing present is simply to resist eternity, for this concentration on the passing present requires a series of quick grasps in time—essential for the centaur level but beside the point with unity consciousness. For the eternal present is *this* moment *before* you try to grasp it. It's what you know before you know anything else, what you see before you see anything else, what you are before you are anything else. To try to grasp it requires a move; to try not to grasp it also requires a move. Either way, he misses it right off.

At this point in his quest, the individual starts to feel hemmed in on all sides. Nothing he can do seems right. To halt resisting, he still has to resist. To seek the timeless now requires a split second of time. To stop moving away, he still has to make a move. And so it slowly starts to dawn on him that *everything he does is a resistance.* It is not that he sometimes resists and sometimes doesn't, but that (as long as he recognizes time and is aware of a separate self) he is *only* resisting and moving away. *All* he is ever doing is moving away. And this includes all his clever attempts not to move away. He cannot, in truth, make a move without resisting because every *move* is, by definition, resistance itself.

On each of the upper levels of the spectrum, there was some action which, by the standards of that particular level, was not a resistance. For example, free association on the ego level and attention to the passing present on the centaur level were not resistances, at least not in the framework of those levels. In all of these cases, a person could therefore choose to resist, or choose not to resist. He had alternatives. There was his self on the one hand (persona, ego, centaur, or transpersonal), and his resistance on the other.

But here, at the base of the spectrum, these is no alternative. Therapy on every upper level was the overthrowing of a gross resistance by strengthening a subtler one. But here there is no subtler resistance. The individual no longer has an alternative to resistance, for everything he does *is* resistance. He has chased resistance to the limit of the spectrum, and here it encloses him.

And there is a special reason for this, which he begins to intuit. His separate self always seems to be resisting because the sensation of the separate self and the sensation of resistance are one and the same thing. That inner feeling of being a separate self is nothing but a feeling of moving away, resisting, contracting, standing aside, looking away, grasping. When you feel yourself, that's all you feel.

This is the reason that everything he tried to do, or tried not to do, was "wrong," was just more resistance and more moving away. Everything he did was wrong because *he* was doing it. His self *is* resistance, and thus could not stop resistance.

At this point, things indeed seem bleak. The individual seems nothing but a trap set to perpetually snare himself. The dark night of the soul sets in, and the light of consciousness seems to turn back on itself and disappear, leaving no trace. All seems lost, and, in a sense, all is. Darkness follows darkness, emptiness leads to emptiness, midnight lingers on. But, as the *Zenrin* has it:

> At dusk the cock announces dawn;
> At midnight, the bright sun.

For reasons we will soon explain, at this very point where absolutely everything seems wrong, everything spontaneously becomes right. When the individual truly sees that every move he makes is a move *away,* a resistance, then the entire machination of resistance winds down. When he sees this resistance in every move he makes, then, quite spontaneously he surrenders resistance altogether. And the surrendering of this resistance is the opening of unity consciousness, the actualization of no-boundary awareness. He awakens, as if from a long and foggy dream, to find what he knew all along: he, as a separate self, does not exist. His real self, the All, was never born, will never die. There is only Consciousness as Such in all directions, absolute and all-pervading, radiant through and as all conditions, the source and suchness of everything that arises moment to moment, utterly prior to this world but not other than this world. All things are just a ripple in this pond; all arising is a gesture of this one.

We have seen, then, that the special conditions of spiritual practice show the individual all of his resistances, while simultaenously frustrating them at the very deepest levels. In short, the conditions show us our wave-jumping, and then make it finally impossible. The turning point comes when the person sees that *everything* he does is nothing but wave-jumping, resisting, moving away from now in search of wetter waves. Spiritual practice, whether a person realizes it in these terms or not, hinges on this primal pivot.

For until he sees that absolutely *everything* he does is resistance, he will secretly continue to move away, to grasp, to seek, and thus to totally prevent the discovery. He will move away without realizing he is moving away. If he doesn't see that *all* his actions are resistances, he will still believe there is some move he can make to get unity consciousness. Until he sees that everything he does is nothing but a moving away, he will simply continue to move away. He will think he has a choice, an alternative, something to do, some way out. And so he continues to make a move—a move which is always *away*—and thus a move that erects a barrier to unity consciousness which was *not* there to begin with. The reason he doesn't "get" unity consciousness is because he wants to.

But at the very point he sees that everything he does is a resistance, a looking away and moving away, then he has no choice but to surrender. He cannot, however, *try* to do this, or try not to! We have seen that doesn't work at all, for both tries are just more movings-away. Rather, it happens of itself, spontaneously, when he *sees* that nothing he can do, or not do, will work, because unity is always already the case. The very seeing of the resistance is the dissolution of the resistance, and acknowledgment of the prior unity.

Once this primal resistance begins to dissolve, one's separate self dissolves with it. For it is not that you, on the one hand, see your moving away, on the other. It might start this way, with you as a separate self seeing the resistance as an activity of yours. But as you begin to see that everything you do is a resistance, you start to see that even your feeling of being a separate self "in here" is also nothing but a resistance. When you feel yourself, all you feel is a tiny inner tension, a subtle contraction, a subtle moving away. The feeling of self and the feeling of moving away are one and the same. But as this becomes obvious, there are no longer *two* different feelings here, no longer an experiencer on the one hand having an experience on the other hand, but only one, single, all-pervasive feeling—the feeling of resistance. You don't feel this resistance, you *are* this feeling of resistance. The feeling of self condenses into the feeling of resistance, and both dissolve.

Thus, to the extent this primal resistance dissolves, your separation from the world also dissolves. There spontaneously comes a deep and total surrender of resistance, of the unwillingness to gaze upon the present in all its forms, and thus a complete dissolution of the primary boundary you erected between inside and outside. When you no longer are resisting present experience, you no longer have a motive to separate yourself from it. The world and the self return as one single experience, not two different ones. No longer do we wave-jump, for there's only one wave, and it's everywhere.

Further, when we are no longer moving away from experience, experience no longer seems to move past us. To no longer resist the present is to see that there is nothing but the present—no beginning, no end, nothing behind it, nothing in front of it. When the past of memory and the future of anticipation are both seen to be present facts, then the slats to this present collapse. The boundaries *around* this moment fall *into* this moment, and then there is nothing but this moment, with nowhere else to go. Said an old Zen master:

My self of long ago,
In nature non-existent;
Nowhere to go when dead,
Nothing at all.

It thus becomes apparent why the search for unity consciousness was so exasperating. Everything we tried to do was wrong because everything was already and eternally right. Even what appeared as a primal resistance to Brahman was actually a movement of Brahman, because there is *nothing but* Brahman. There never was, nor will there ever be, any time other than Now. What appeared as that primal moving *away* from Now was really an original movement *of* Now. *Honsho-myoshu.* Original enlightenment *is* wondrous practice. The eternal Now *is* its movements. The ocean waves surge freely against the shore, wetting the pebbles and shells.

RECOMMENDATIONS

For the Hindu approach, one can do no better than the illustrious Sri Ramana Maharshi. Arthur Osborne has collected most of his works, and edited them into superb volumes. See especially *The Collected Works of Ramana Maharshi* (London: Riber, 1959) and *Teachings of Ramana Maharshi* (London: Rider, 1962).

For the Buddhist approach, we have three main lines. For the Theravadin or early Buddhism, see Nyaniponika Thera, *The Heart of Buddhist Meditation* (London: Rider, 1972). For Vajrayana, or Tibetan Buddhism, Chögyam Trungpa's books are illuminating, especially *Cutting Through Spiritual Materialism* (Berkeley: Shambhala, 1973) and *The Myth of Freedom* (Berkeley: Shambhala, 1976). Excellent material by Tarthang Tulku can be found in issues of *The Crystal Mirror*. For the Zen approach, see the entire series of writings coming out of the Zen Center of Los Angeles—*The Hazy Moon of Enlightenment, The Way of Everyday Life, To Forget the Self.* Suzuki Roshi's *Zen Mind, Beginner's*

Mind (New York: Weatherhill, 1970) is a masterpiece; and Philip Kapleau's *The Three Pillars of Zen* (Boston: Beacon, 1965) remains a small classic.

Two other approaches should be mentioned, neither of which is traditional. Krishnamurti, whose insights we have freely drawn on in this book, eloquently speaks through his many works, of which *The First and Last Freedom* (Wheaton: Quest, 1954) and *Commentaries on Living* (3 volumes) (Wheaton: Quest, 1968) may be especially mentioned. The works of Bubba Free John are unsurpassed. See *The Enlightenment of the Whole Body* (Middletown: Dawn Horse Press, 1978).

These approaches—or ones similar—seem to me the only ones both strong and gentle enough to elicit true understanding in the midst of present activity. Real spiritual practice is not something we do for twenty minutes a day, for two hours a day, or for six hours a day. It is not something we do once a day in the morning, or once a week on Sunday. Spiritual practice is not one activity among other human activities; it is the ground of all human activities, their source and their validation. It is a prior commitment to Transcendent Truth lived, breathed, intuited, and practiced twenty-four hours a day. To intuit your real self is to commit your entire being to the actualization of that self in all beings, according to the primordial vow: "However innumerable beings are, I vow to liberate them; however incomparable the Truth is, I vow to actualize it." If you feel this deep commitment to realization, to service, to sacrifice, and to surrender, through all present conditions to infinity itself, then spiritual practice will be your way naturally. May you be graced to find a spiritual master in this life and enlightenment in this moment.

Index